Folklore and Its Motifs in Modern Literature

Folklore and its Motifs in Modern Literature

Dr Kishore Jadav

Manas Publications
(We Convert Fighters into Writers)
New Delhi-110002 (INDIA)

MANAS PUBLICATIONS
(We Convert Fighters into Writers)
(Publishers, Library Suppliers, Importers & Exporters)
4402/5-A, Ansari Road (Opp. HDFC Bank)
Darya Ganj, New Delhi-110 002 (India)
Off. (23260783, 23265523, Fax: 011-23272766
E-mail: manaspublications@gmail.com
manaspublications@yahoo.com

ISBN 81-7049-086-3
₹ 700/-

Designed at
Manas Publications

Printed in India at
HS Offsets, Delhi
and published by Mrs Suman Lata for
Manas Publications, 4402/5-A,
Ansari Road, (Opp. HDFC Bank),
Darya Ganj, New Delhi-110 002 (INDIA)

To
my mother

Preface

Folklore is a wide-ranging expression of rich and complex, archaic culture. It is a vital element of a living culture. It represents the ancient thought of mankind, their feelings and worldview, their shared experiences and wisdom.

The North Eastern region of India is endowed with rich folklore material which, due to its diverse aspects, has not been systematically studied nor scientifically analysed till recently. However, it is my privilege to intimately know the hill races, and imbibe their labyrinthine social practices, religious ethos and cultural characteristics by living in the tribal milieu, cultivating close rapport with them, and sharing their life for upwards of thirty-five years during the most turbulent period. My efforts to present a study on the myths, folktales, songs, lyrics, legends, rites and rituals, some of the performing arts, and to a certain extent illustrative customs and traditions of the major tribes of North East India could take the concrete shape of a book, thanks to the opportunity provided to me to present the inaugural address at the national seminar on 'Interpreting Literature in Tribal Languages and Oral Traditions', organised at Tejgadh (Baroda) under the auspices of Sahitya Akademi, New Delhi, in 1996. The three-day workshop witnessed series of in-depth discussions by scholars from different parts of the country which underlined the growing importance of the studies in folk literature and folk culture.

My approach in this book has not been confined just to the academic study of a particular tribe and its cultural life. But, I have embarked upon studying most of the selective and significant items (aspects) of traditional lores and divergent cultural patterns prevailing in large areas of North East

India, bringing out the wide ranging variations within their social structure and value system.

In my critical evaluation of folklore, I have resorted to mythological, morphological, structural, psychoanalytical and humanistic interpretations. My articles on various disciplines viz., Indology, Philosophy, Religion, Culture, History and Literature, attempt to focus on the closely related fields of Ethnology and Social Anthropology without slipping into pedantic abstraction. I have kept in mind not only the scholars, but also the common reader to make the book accessible to him to understand the richness and complexities of human life.

After all, not the lengthy and cumbersome disquisition, but the life-song itself often gives us a clearer insight into a people's soul. In order to reinforce this point, an extensive treatment has been given to the chapter on folk songs wherein lie certain important clues to the philosophy of life. While portraying various themes, the qualitative details of their life cycle have been highlighted. Numerous different and mutually not understandable dialects are spoken in the North–East, and this rich linguistic diversity coincides with the great cultural diversity in the region. Nevertheless, the comparison of the divergent cultural patterns would reveal that there exists a common bond of homogeneous character as far as their unique modes of living, customs and ideas of a singular people living in the most beautiful part of India, are concerned.

This painstaking work tries to present a cohesive view of the tribal people's psyche, their religious and spiritual phantasies, ritual practices, exuberant dances, songs and games, and their colourfully woven textiles. Even as it is, this book can hardly claim to be a comprehensive study of all the aspects of their folk culture. The possibility always remains that some important aspects of their culture which should not have been missed, may have actually been overlooked, notwithstanding the fact that most dominant and representative items have been selected from different parts of the region.

An additional dimension requires to be added to the practice of head-hunting, the folk tale of which is syntagmatically analysed in the book. Although head-hunting had been banned in some parts of Konyak area under British administration, its traditions and meaning were very much alive till the middle of the twentieth century. And, to this day, the appropriate method of propitiating the terrible goddess Kali, (who is also Durga, 'hard of approach'), is by bloody sacrifices. The Saiva or Sakta form of Hinduism that came into being in Kama-rupa would therefore seem to be due to engrafting of Koch superstitions on the purer and humane religious ideas propagated in India by the Aryan settlers. From this point of view, it is important to recall that the Garos were head-hunters almost until the end of nineteenth century, and that the Chutiyas were conspicuous, in the North-East, for their addiction to human sacrifice.

Another focus of reader's attention is the description of courtship and pre-marital and extra-marital amorous relations prevalent in certain tribal societies. Even by Western moral standards, they appear to be quite free in this respect. Nevertheless, such sexual behaviour before marriage and outside of wedlock is governed by group membership and by standards of propriety that are very different from those customary in the Western culture. It has been made abundantly clear as to how sexual behaviour is culturally patterned, limited and restricted. For our understanding, these balances between freedom and restraint are of great importance, since some form of them is an integral part of all human cultures.

Now, *all* aspects of tribal life in the North Eastern region have changed drastically, initiating a process of social and cultural disintegration. The traditional form of tribal life has been disrupted and the spectrum of multi-dimensional social changes have brought its total transformation. The folk culture is slowly being overtaken by the present technological age. Of course, its dying process is very slow. Because, any item of folk literature is completely lost only when it ceases to exist in the memory of man. The purpose of this study is to document such disappearing phase of ancient life for the posterity to which, perhaps, its certain original descriptions may appear naive and extravagantly romantic.

I have devoted the final chapter to demonstrate the range of adaptation of folklore's modes and motifs - its structures and themes, and even its characters - in the modern short story by the practising masters of this genre, particularly in Western and European literature. The short story is the form most congenial to its Spartan aesthetic. Despite short story's various experimental phases - dream and magic realism, sur-realism and irrealism, tremendous assortment of minimalism, and maximalism too - its brevity of form has helped sustaining kinship with oral narrative throughout past two centuries, especially by infusing it with vital folk elements bringing new vigor, to this art. This dimension, perhaps, is a special allure for the scholars in both literary and folkloristic studies.

It will be observed that the illustrations are not referred to in the body of the work. However, they form unconspicuously an integral part of the book, with an unwritten chapter on the tribal folk dances rendering an illustrative visual documentation. I contemplate to bring out a separate volume on these aspects covering visual folk arts and folk dances of the North Eastern region, in due course.

My first contact with the tribal people of the North East dates back to 1963 when the State of Nagaland was undergoing formation process. It was my good fortune to take up an assignment with Mr. M.L. Kampani, IAS (Rtd), then Deputy Commissioner, Mokokchung and later Lt.Governor, Andaman and Nicobar, and Advisor to the Governor of Nagaland, as his Personal Assistant to accompany him on several official tours to the interiors, even on foot where there were no jeepable roads, to the highest posts such as Chudi, Topsu, Meraktsu, Lotsu, Ralan in Lotha area. Though the journey used to be arduous, it was infinitely rewarding. Since then, I had extensively travelled in the whole of North Eastern region, right across the Burmese border, during my service career while holding responsible and important assignments, with Mr. S.C. Dev, IAS (Rtd), then Commissioner of Nagaland, who has authored 'Nagaland : the Untold Story', Mr. I.Longkumer, IAS(Rtd), then Chief Secretary of the State, and several other political dignitaries.

Whenever my main preoccupation permitted me any leisure, I utilised it on research and writings (creative works and criticism) on Literature, Philosophy, and Culture etc.. I have published seventeen books in the past thirty years. Some of them carry collections of short stories, articles on its art and aesthetics, interviews and novels. Three of my books had also been prescribed as text-books in post-graduate programme (MA) for two-three terms in South Gujarat and Gujarat universities. A few Post Graduate scholars have received their Ph.D. by undertaking research and dissertations on my works.

The present volume is a part of my current research project focussing on the larger aspects of north-eastern folk culture. Wading through several vicissitudes and upheavals, the region is now thriving in all-round prosperity, rushing into the stream of modern life. With the rapid progress resulting in material and socio-psychic development, the changes in life style and acculturation have brought forth a tribal identity crisis. Therefore, it is left to the competent intellectual elite to form their own opinion as to the relevance of this study based on a scholar author's own experience, under the present circumstances.

I wish to acknowledge my deep debt of gratitude to those friends and distant people relegated to the past who initiated me into this land three decades ago and extended exceptional help in shaping my destiny. It is my duty to thank those who have been good enough to stand by me at the hour of my trials and tribulations, particularly during my ordeal, so that I have been able to dedicate myself to this intellectual task. I am also grateful to my University staff who provided me the computer assistance in the preparation of this volume.

I am especially indebted to Manas Publications, Delhi who wholeheartedly accepted to convert my study into fine print for the wider readership, strengthening the bond of our friendship.

Dr. Kishore Jadav

Contents

List of Illustrations

Yimchunger folk dance (Nagaland)

Zeliang folk dance (Nagaland)

Sema Tuluni festival folk dance (Nagaland)

Sangtam Amongmong festival folk dance (Nagaland)

Ao folk dance (Nagaland)

A traditional dance of Tagin Si-Donyi festival (Arunachal Pradesh)

Ponung folk dance (Arunachal Pradesh)

Kherai folk dance of Bodos (Assam)

Deori Bihu festival folk dance (Assam)

The Boisagu festival folk dance (Assam)

Wangla folk dance of Garos (Meghalaya)

A traditional Banai folk dance (Meghalaya and Assam)

Radha in Ras Lila (Manipur)

Krishna in Ras Lila (Manipur)

Nagas with the log drum (Nagaland)

Angami gate pulling (Nagaland)

Chapter 1

Introduction

The 'Tribal Literature and Oral Tradition" forms a major and integral part of the folk literature, i.e. folklore. Since no specific term has been coined so far to categorise this aspect of tribal wealth into a distinct category or a separate grouping for its exclusive study, it will be a futile attempt to tear it apart from the vast spectrum of folklore and its conceptual frame-work. Further, a question arises as to who are the folk? 'Folk' is synonymous with people. This term is defined succinctly in Webster's New Collegiate Dictionary (8th edition) :

"The great proportion of the members of a people that determines the group character and that tends to preserve its characteristic form of civilization and its customs, arts and crafts, legends, traditions, and superstitions from generation to generation."

Therefore, it is intended here to go with the current usage of this term and to undertake interpretations of folklore (special reference to North East of India) with the tools available to us.

Folk literature is the lore of unlettered peoples transmitted by word of mouth. It consists, as does written literature, of both prose and verse narratives,poems and songs, myths, dramas, rituals, proverbs, riddles and the like. Until about 4000 BC, all literature was folk literature. But writing developed in the years between 4000 and 3000 BC, in both Egypt and the Mesopotamian civilization at Sumer.

Thereafter from Asia, North Africa and the Meditarranean lands spread rapidly the written literature over much of the world. Nevertheless, during all these centuries when the world was learning how to write, there still existed a large and important activity carried on by those actually unlettered and not much used to reading and writing. Even now, majority of men and women on earth are still carrying the tradition of oral folk literature, since it's the only kind they know.

Each group of people has handled its folk literature in its own way, and neither its origin nor its evolution can be explicitly spoken of. Its transmission from person to person and its exposure to various influences that affect it consciously or unconsciously has brought about its constant change. In the process, some items may find improvement and develop in to a new literary form or may die out from the oral repertory due to overwhelming alien influences. The skilled practitioners of the tradition, storytellers or epic singers have preserved their literary expression in the memory of folk. Though, the classical composers of written literature in 16th and 17th century had borrowed tales and motifs from oral narratives and forgotten their folk origins, these stories in their literary form have often lived side by side with the tales told by oral storytellers. Children also play an important role in carrying on certain kinds of oral tradition such as singing games, riddles, and dance songs. These are passed from generation to generation by word of mouth and enriched by continuous additions, always remain within the oral tradition. Even though books, radio and television etc. have replaced folk literature, in the present day urbanised culture it is still, as it has always been, the normal literary expression for the unlettered peoples of all continents.

The most obvious characteristic of folk literature is the fact that it is oral. The continued existence of an item of oral literature depends upon memory. It thus happens that in nearly all cultures, certain people specialize in remembering and repeating what they have heard. There are some semi-professional storytellers around whom large groups of people gather in bazars, or before cottage-fires or in leisure hours after labour. They possess prodigious memories and with slight variations, from time to time, they pass on to a new generation hundreds of tales and traditions that they heard long ago. Certain bards, minstrels and songmakers develop special techniques of singing or narrating epic or heroic tales to the accompaniment of a harp or other musical instruments. In the course of time, at various places, special poetic forms have been perfected and passed on from bard to bard. In this way, remarkably skilful heroic meters of the Greek epics were developed out of the oral stream of narratives which after suffering many strange changes, eventually, ceased to be oral literature and are now enshrined in manuscripts and books. Elaborate religious rituals and the ideal of establishing relation of man with the higher powers carried on by religious leaders through generations have perpetuated the oral tradition of folk literature.

Chapter 2

Folklore : Conceptual Frame-Work

Folk literature is but a part of folklore. Customs and beliefs, ritualistic behaviour, dances, folk music and other non-literary manifestations form part of the larger study of ethnology. However, these distinctions are of concern to the folklorists. The term 'folklore' was first coined by William Thoms, a British antiquarian in 1846. The study of folklore materials was, at that time, being carried on under labels such as 'Popular Antiquities' or 'Popular Literature'. Therefore, he suggested 'a good Saxon Compound Folk-lore—the lore of the people.' Besides, the work of Brothers Grimm, particularly German Philologist Jacob Grimm (1785–1863) who published the first volume (1812-14) of the 'Kinder Und Mausmarchen' (translated as Grimms' Fairy Tales), the scholarly scientific study on folklore was initiated. The *Marchen*, or Tales were the detritus of the old myths. Ofcourse, all the American folklore-minded anthropologists experienced difficulty in employing the term folklore within a culture almost wholly oraland traditional, and they resorted to various substitutes : William Bascom, a student of Herskouvits, suggested the term 'verbal art' to denote the oral aesthetic tradition of tale, proverb, song, and riddle in the culture, tearing out the supernatural belief-system and the plastics. He clarified the functional uses of folklore in nonliterate societies.

In order to trace the growth of folkloristic studies, we must focus on the scholarly works done in Asia, particularly in India, before the Grimms' Fairy Tales viz., *Kathasaritsagar, Panchatantra* and *Jataks*. A German scholar, Theodor Benfey, even claimed in his introduction to *Panchatantra* (1859) that India, the seat of an ancient, highly developed civilisation that had spread to Europe, was the home of the master tales subsequently found in the Grimms' collection. Along with language and mythology, these wonder tales had diffused from India to Europe in ancient and historic times along well-traversed trade routes. The famous 'Historical-Geographical' School known as Finnish School was highly inspired by this diffusionist theory. Some scholars in India applied the methodology of this formalistic discipline in their studies while Benfey's theory gave support to mythological perspective. However, European scholars (with strong colonial convictions) including famous indologists, historians and anthropologists who believed in gradually converting India and bringing it within the Greek/Roman/Semitic culture zone, discarded the diffusionist approach and advocated theories that were ploygenetic in nature.

Anthropologists of the School of Cambridge University converged on a central idea of myth-ritual origins of folklore on the basis of comparative study of Sir James George Frazer (The Golden Bough, 1st edition 1890). In their view, mythic narrative accompanied and explained a sacrificial fertility ritual among the heathens. In course of time, the myth becomes separated from the rite and floats independently in oral tradition, to splinter into magic tales, popular ballads, nursery rhymes and other folklore genres.

Partly as a result of the romantic movement in literature and partly due to the interest in primitivism and the common folk, the recording of all sorts of songs and oral tales has been phenomenal since about 1800. Scholars have propounded many theories about the origin, development, spread and structure of folklore throughout the world in the last (more than) 150 years. Besides, 'comparative mythology' developed by Max Muller on his publication of translated version from the Sanskrit 'Sacred Books of the East'. 'Evolutionary' theory of culture and 'devolutionary' theory of folklore which emerged in a hypothesis put forward by Theodor Benfey, and several other Schools also engaged themselves in the studies and interpretation of folklore. To name a few :

1. Mythological School
2. Migrational/Benfey's School
3. Anthropological School
4. Historical-Geographical/'Finnish' School
5. Psychoanalytical School
6. Structural School
   a) Syntagmatic/Propp's Morphological School
   b) Paradigmatic/Levi Straushian School
7. Thompsonian Concept of Motif/Classificatory analysis-tale-types
8. Functional School
9. Historical reconstructional theory
10. Ideological theory
11. Oral Formulaic theory
12. Cross-Cultural theory
13. Folk-cultural theory
14. Mass-cultural theory
15. Contextual theory
16. Hemispheric theory

It is beyond the scope of this book to go into details and judge the validity of these methodologies. These are just mentioned to underline the special importance due to this field of learning today in a world where traditional values, cultural traits and human virtues are overwhelmed by modern ideas and values of an electronic age. The writers and lyricists have always used themes taken from oral legends and folk songs, and in turn have themselves affected the traditions. In the recent years, cinema has presented old folk-tales to an enthralling public, and special interest in the folk songs has been stimulated by radio and television. Inevitably, this oral literature has become less truly oral, and mostly pseudo-folk culture has been presented to the public. Therefore, during the past few generations folk-festivals have flourished in both number and rich variety, and have become almost worldwide. They have been like a stimulus of preservation of a *disappearing phase of modern life,* and are likely to revive older dances keeping them within the authentic local traditions. The inquiring minds of intellectuals in Social Sciences and Humanities—particularly ethnologists, anthropologists, historians etc. have adopted scientific approach to investigate this subject of a substantial, worldwide body of scholarship.

Even the psychologists have provided non-formalistic folkloristic theory based on interpretation of folklore in terms of symbolically Oedipus complex and sexual imagery discovered by Sigmund Freud ; while Eric Fromm and Hungary-born Gaza Roheim analysed the tales, myths and dreams in terms of psycho-analytical perceptions, Austrian psychoanalytic folklorists equated dream as the myth of the individuals and, therefore, applied the same mechanism for the interpretation of dreams, and myths and folk-tales. On the assumption of dream as individual myth, and myth as social dream, the myths revealed the psychic childhood repressions of a whole race or culture.

In India, we always talk of *Marg* and *Desi, Vaidic* and *Laukik* i.e. classical and folk traditions, which is rechristened as Great and Little traditions. Unilinear evolutions and few universals may not explain the variety produced by multi-culture folk traditions. In this sense, the Indian equivalent of folklore, '*lokayana*' coined by Suniti Kumar Chatterji, expresses the real scope of folklore as it signified a way of life (*yana*) of a people (*lok*). The area of folklore is, therefore, circumscribed by a pedagogical motive of adjusting the members of a social group to the needs of the group. Folklore thus ultimately becomes the means of expression of a group's own attitude and cultural life. The civilization of a people being a movement from unconscious to conscious, it is obvious that their beliefs and customs would be didactic with an end to adjust man to his immediate surroundings for a leap forward to his future. Ultimately, the said area would give us a glimpse of social formations, cultural evolutions and the group's world view.

In the colonized nations, each folk tradition serves to reinforce the group identity of its members in a pluralistic culture. Syncretism, acculturation or the fusion of different traditions is a process especially characteristic of new world folklore. The traditional lore physically attached to the original homeland seems to vanish fast. If any of its items cease to exist within the memory of man, it is completely lost. However, its dying process is actually very slow. Tribal peoples scattered across different continents need their myths to safeguard their identity. Therefore, in the electronic age, according to Marshall McLuhan, the literate world is reverting to an oral-aural community.

Before we embark upon interpreting the tribal lore, let us consider the concept of this genre-folklore. Of course, genre-definition has its own pitfalls, since attempts at clear categorisation invariably slice off the related forms. Serious students and academicians, by no means, agree on the boundaries of their discipline. Although it is difficult to suggest a ready-made frame-work in which varying aspects of various cultures or nations can be fixed, there does exist an internationally accepted format which, with a little modification, can be followed in respect of each culture or nation. The elusive materials of folklore can be best defined through the formal genres into which they fall. Four broad sectors of folklore and folklife studies, as given below, have been outlined by scholars :

1. Oral literature
2. Material Culture
3. Social Customs and festivals
4. Performing folk-Art.

Oral Literature : Oral literature, also called as verbal art or expressive literature are 'spoken, sung and voiced forms of traditional utterances'. Oral narrative is one big sub-division of this group, which in turn has its own manifold distinctions. For example, myth, fairy-tale or *marchen,* romantic tale or novella, religious tale, folktale, legend, animal tale, anecdote, joke, numskull tale etc. Another major sub-division of oral literature is oral poetry or folk poetry which has its own family of related forms i.e. folk epics, ballads, folk songs, lullabies, work songs, 'Deh-bichar' songs, 'Zikirs' (with reference to the North East of India) and songs associated with rituals and rites (Samskaras), of birth, marriage, death, etc, commonly found in almost all parts of India. Also included in this category is the rich oral poetry connected with festive occasions, feasts and ceremonies. Proverbs embodying wisdom in pithy phrases and riddles with enigmatic question paired with a deceptive answer still function in folk/tribal societies as important devices for imparting knowledge about cultural semantics, logical and behavioural patterns among the younger members. The folk speech embraces the local and regional turns of phrase that deviate from the standard language, which are sometimes taboo words or expressions from passive vocabulary. Characteristics at the level of grammar, idiom and even phonetics and nonsense sentence - of such slang is difficult to pronounce because of its string of assonances. In this category, minor forms viz. beliefs or superstitions, chants, prayers, laments and cries can also be enumerated.

Material Culture : In the spectrum of folklore, material culture or folklife responds to techniques, skills, recipes, and formulas transmitted across the generations and, it is subject to the same forces of traditions and individual variations as verbal art, which is visual rather than aural. In this category can be placed folk architecture, arts and crafts, designs and decorations of the buildings and utensils, and performance of home industries according to traditional styles and methods. Decorative paintings embellishing the walls and entrances of rural/tribal homes having both ritualistic and aesthetic significance is a pan-Indian phenomenon. Although the motifs of such paintings of one region or culture zone may vary from that of another, their structural unity remains the same. For instance, the snake and sparrow motifs are predominant in South and East coasts; and animal, tree and flower motifs are common in Northern tribes.

Social Customs and Festivals : Here the emphasis is on group interaction rather than on individual skills and performances. To the verbal and tangible elements are added group behavioural traits. Of particular importance are the *rites de passage* such as birth, initiation, marriage, death and similar paraphernalia. Rituals and customs associated with festivals in our country are sometimes related to agricultural activity following a calendrical cycle. These along with customs associated with religious practices and the concept of Indian world-view form an important segment of folklife, and they partly function to provide psychic reassurance against external dangers of natural calamities. The religious aspect is multi-dimensional encompassing the most complex caste hierarchy which has a net-work of inter-relations with the religious hierarchy. Besides pan-Indian mode of worshipping Hindu pantheon, there are very ancient and indigenous modes of worship and performance of rites prevalent in tribal belts to placate gods and demons, quite distinguishable from other parts of the country.

Performing Folk-Art : This sector of folklore studies concerns primarily with the traditional music, drama and dance passed on to the succeeding generations by ear and performed by memory rather than by the written and printed musical score and relevant literature, which usually overcome the generic barriers. The folk-music is 'functional' in the sense that it is not entertainment or of particular aesthetic interest, but is an accompaniment to other activities. It is typically disseminated within families and restricted to social networks. Though rural in nature, it exists in cultures in which there is technically more sophisticated musical tradition and, it is perpetuated and venerated as a spontaneous creation by ethnic, occupational or religious minorities unencumbered by artistic self-consciousness and aesthetic theories. Folk music is an embodiment of the common experience of inhabitants of the locale to promote self-esteem, self-preservation and social solidarity. Though folk music is not merely a debased art music nor an essential component of the latter, a symbiotic relationship appears to have been established by it to other music forms popular in the larger society of which the folk/tribal community is a part.

Folk music is closely related to popular music in several ways. Societies possessing popular music also have a folk/tribal tradition, or remnants thereof. The partial duplication of repertories and styles indicate a cross-fertilization between the two music forms, and both tended to merge in the twentieth century. Folk-rock interaction, American Jaaz, rhythm and blues, country western music, and Latin American forms such as tango and bossa nova are fine illustrations. The terms 'folk/tribal' and 'popular' are two points on a musical continuum, rather than discrete bodies of music. From a sociological point of view, the folk and popular music have less in common. Popular music, an ephemeral commercial product, is produced by professionals for consumption by an urban, non-participating mass audience. And its production, vital criteria of folk-music (i.e. oral tradition, communal recreation, etc.) are not operative.

Folk music has not only influenced popular music in India, but also some of the classical forms of music due to the fact that it possesses hidden potential for the sake of theoretical purpose. At times, a particular kind of folk music is identifiable only by its instruments and is passed from one generation to another. Such traditions are known by the name of instruments viz., *Ladisah* of Kashmir, *Pena* of Manipur tribe, *Kamsale* of Karnataka.

Many scholars trained in ethnomusicology, a discipline concerned with elucidating music in a cross-cultural perspective, considered folk music as a repository of archaisms—a legacy from which the prehistory of language, literature and other cultural traits could be adduced.

The origin of folk dances may be very ancient and they may have grown out of creative inspiration, and they continue to sprout from the imagination of individuals and groups, people of all classes who sense the traditions and the aspirations of their environment. In the Indian subcontinent, such dance forms have survived, whose origins can be traced back to pre-historic times and places, from which new forms have grown up in other places. The buoyant tenacity with which the dance forms have continued in spite of many momentous historical, sociological changes present a bewilderingly rich and complex phenomenon. Both folk dances and highly sophisticated classical dances have not only influenced each other but also nourished each other. The distinction has been blurred in such ever-changing and floating conditions that it could be a illusion to claim that one can hold on to a distinct-line; but in viewing the entire spectacular phenomenon of continuities, changes, mutation and transformation and forward-back-forward steps with rhapsody, for these are so essential for a living civilization that India is.

The tribal dances in the country retain their originality, simplicity and spontaneity, be it *Kimbu* or *Zeling* of the Nagas, *Laho* of the Jaintias, *Wanglas* of the Garos, *Dimasa* of the Kacharis, or *Lai-Haraba* of the Meithis. The Assamese Bihu dances with Bihu songs (specially during Bohag-Bihu spring festival) linking them with many tribal communities of North East India are performed accompanied by instruments like drum, cymbal, gagana (Jew's harp), bamboo clapper and horn-pipe.

Considering dances as a manifestation of rituals and entertainments, the English scholar Douglas Keneddy has rightly pointed out that when primitive religion weakens, some of the mystery and the magic departs from the dances that express it. The dancer becomes less a medicine-maker and more a performing artist as ritual changes imperceptibly into art. In short, man's social adjustment to the environment, for purposes of survival, created both the original dance rituals and their subsequent functional or formal changes. Vestigial animal dances echo ancient animistic rites. For example, the Ainu tribes of northern Japan still mime bear and fox hunts, portraying the animals realistically. In West Africa, an antelope hunt in dance has ritualistic overtones, while monkey mimes are for entertainment alone. Male combat dances of the Balkans echo ancient pre-Christian rites for initiation into brotherhoods, the heralding of spring and of animal fecundity, and healing.

In other parts of the world, folk/tribal dances are shifting from man-deity and man-nature purpose to a man-man or male-female attitude according to the changes in the beliefs and in methods of producing the essentials of life. This has led to creating numerous adjustments and adaptation to ecology to a basis in Christian festivals and the resultant shifts in the organization of dance groups.

In recent years, the folk drama has helped the theoretical growth both in anthropology and folkloristics, so much so that an eminent researcher like Peacock believes that semantic aspects of cultural change and the cosmological categories of human societies can be accurately deciphered through drama, particularly through folk drama. In the esoteric dance rituals of Australia, in the mythological dance enactments of India and Indonesia, in Nigeria and in its distant New World derivatives such as the Vodum dance is immersed in the larger drama of the rite. The symbolism of song texts, the traditional music, and the meaning of masks and costumes, not to speak of the setting in a sacred grove here and there, the decorative invocations to animistic spirits have survived mysteriously. Needless to mention here that a characteristic feature of folk drama is that it differs from the written/recorded drama in performance-audience relationship and also in mode of transmission.

The most striking and fascinating feature of folk-drama is that the music and dance have close affinity with this form and is associated with rituals and festivals and bear resemblances to the movable village-drama of African tribes. Both these elements are contained in what is now lebelled as dance-drama which is recognised as a kind of new genre, viz., *Tamasha* of Maharashtra, *Yakshagana* of Karnataka, *Kathakali* of Kerala. In the fixed-stage theatrical performance of classical tradition type, like Radha-Krishna enactment of Manipur tribal dance, based on the life of Krishna, the young women use simplified gestures evolved from the large, complex system of hand-gestures known as *mudras.* The basic gestural symbols are derived from the wrist position, the position of the palm, and the poses of the fingers. Each gesture has its prescribed musical instrument. A trembling leaf, for example, is symbolised by the *alapalava,*—a rotation of the wrist accompanied by the folding and unfolding of the fingers.

Here regional variations include preferences for mime or for abstract movements, respectfully graceful and comic, creating a most impressive scenario of beauty and grandeur. Such folk art need to be viewed holistically rather than fixing it in *a priori* western genre-model.

References

1. Dundes Alan (ed.), The Study of Folklore, New Jersey, Prentice Hall, 1965.
2. ——-Introduction to "The Morphology of theFolk-tale", 2nd edn.,1968.
3. Dorson, Richard M. (ed.), Folklore and Folklife : Introduction, Chicago, University of Chicago Press, 1972.
4. —— American Folklore, 1959.
5. Yonder, Don (ed.), American Folklife, Austin, University of Texas Press, 1976.
6. Bascom, William R. "Folklore and Anthropology," Journal of American Folklore 66, 1953, and "Verbal Art," Journal of American Folklore, 68, 1955.
7. Benfey, Theodore, Panchtantra (in German) Berlin, 1859.
8. Edgerton, Franklin, Panchtantra (tr. from Sanskrit), New Delhi, Orient Paperbacks, 1965.
9. Frazer, J.G. The Golden Bough: A Study in Magic and Religion, 12 Vols., London, 1890.
10. Leach, Maria (ed.), Standard Dictionary of Folklore, Mythology and Legends, New York, Funk and Wagnalls, 1949-50.
11. Maranda, P. and Maranda, E. (ed.), Structural Analysis

of Oral Tradition, Philadelphia; University of Pensylvania Press, 1971.
12. Clarke, Keneth and Mary , Introducing Folklore, New York, Halt, Rinehart & Winston, 1963.
13. Harris, Merwin (ed.), The Rise of Anthropological Theory London, Routledge and Kegan Paul, 1972.
14. Propp, V.J., Morphology of the Folktale, Austin; University of Texas Press, 1968 (2nd edn.).
15. Sokolov, Y.M., Russiana Folklore, New York; Macmillan & Co., 1950.
16. Stith, Thompson, Motif-Index of Folk Literature, 6 Vols., 2nd ed., Bloomington, Indiana University, 1955-58.
17. ———-The Types of the Folktales, 2nd revised ed., FF Communications, 184, Helsinki (Based on A. Arne's original work), 1961.
18. Vatsayayan, Kapila, Traditions of Indian Folk Dance, New Delhi, India Book Co., 1974.
19. Gargi, Balwant, Folk Theatre of India, Seattle, University of Washington Press, 1966.
20. Chatterjee, Suniti Kumar, The Cultural Heritage of India, Vol-I, 1948.

Chapter 3

Motifs and Interpretations

MYTHOLOGICAL INTERPRETATION

Now, after giving a background of the conceptual framework of 'Folklore-Folklife', I intend to proceed with the investigation and interpretation of folklore with particular reference to the North Eastern region of India which is inhabited by a confluence of people, popularly known as tribals living in different stages of under-development. This part of India has immense cultural and linguistic diversity. It is very rich in folklore - both in its quality and quantity, which indisputably forms an invaluable part of the literary, cultural and historical traditions of our country. The folklore of the region is the repository of simple truth, high ideas, grand imagery, naive and unsophisticated expressions, delicate ideas and ethical conceptions of the people of the region. It throws light on the cosmological, ethnographical, socio-economic, political, religio-cultural, philosophical, artistic and aesthetic aspects of the lives of the people.

Perhaps, it will not be incorrect to say that the folklore of the tribals of the North East of India constitutes the bedrock of a higher philosophy, higher literature and history and higher art, with its multiplicity of spoken cognate languages and sharing common cultural frame in Kuki-Chin tribes of Mizoram and Southern Manipur, Apatanis and Nishis of Arunachal Pradesh, while spoken austric languages in Khasis, Jaintias and Garos of Bodo language group having compact indigenous cultural base; of course, Meithei folklore has experienced maximum pan-Indian impact of great tradition and diffusion of folklore traits; Chamka shows a curious blend of Bengali and tribal lore; while Nagas have diverse hermetic languages using *lingua-franca* Nagamese for inter-tribal communication, and have multi-coloured cultural mosaic. Influence of Buddhist culture and literature on Mompas, Membas, Sherdukpans and Khambas on one hand, and Khamtis and Singphos on the other is unmistakable. Their folklore plots, themes and motifs owe their origin to literary Buddhist sources via Tibetan and Burmese heritage. Cross-cultural, cross-linguistic and cross-generic scientific analytical studies of folklore and ethnic data on social structures, values, norms and ethos, belief-system and totems etc. shall help in exploring genesis and growth and wealth of such tribal literature. Their oral traditions offer a projective screen that may illuminate the fantasies of the tribal society and provide glimpses of their tribal mind and meanings of universal nature.

The eternal quest of man to know the truth in the natural surroundings led him to invent myths in which the rudiments of history can be discerned. The purpose of the myth is to explain matter in the science of Pre-Scientific age. Levi Straus considered tales as miniature myths. He maintained that there was no serious reason to isolate tales from myths, though the difference between the two was 'subjectively' felt by a great many societies. That was the precise reason for the existence of 'special terms to distinguish the two genres', though they are not founded on the nature of things. He stressed that the tales in one society might be traced in the myths of another, and vice versa is also true. Further, the same tales, the same characters and the same motifs reappear in the tales and myths of a given populace.

The primitive man was in as much need to explain the course of nature and its vagaries as his civilised counterpart, to be assured of a sense of security against the unpredictability of events. The thought process of the preliterate man is neither prelogical, nor anti-logical, but primarily symbolic having its roots in the unconscious which is mostly elaborated in myths and is concerned with the 'logic of the concrete'. Therefore, we have to depend upon the immediacy of reaction to a concrete situation, rather than to a mental abstraction; we may describe this attitude as 'aesthetic reaction'. The primitive man's reaction to the immediate or to the concrete is quantitative and multi-dimensional. Therefore, the myth can never be interpreted only on one level; myths consist of inter-relationship of several explanatory levels, and are elaborated from direct reaction, they are expressed in imagery as in poetry.

Poets also react to concrete situations and project images. Myths thus invariably are emotional perceptions of experience of truth, expressed in what has been earlier called 'the logic of concrete'. A typical story told by Minyongs (Adi tribe of Arunachal Pradesh) about the first appearance of death in the living land is related here :

Ninur-Botte made an earthen vessel. When it was ready, he picked it up to scrutinise it. But he dropped it and broke it into pieces. He made every effort to collect every piece and put it together, but to no avail. He asked : 'Why can't I mend it? I took so much pain to make it." Doini-Pollo (the Sun-Moon God) said : "You did well to make it, you did ill to break it." Ninur-Botte said, "How was it that I did ill?" Doini-Pollo said, "Because from to-day men will die." That is why men die. Had it been possible to put together what was broken, men would have lived eternally.

Here the primitive philosopher has sought to express his perception in a series of imagery projecting symbols in the process. One of the symbols is his acceptance of the universality and inevitability of death as a natural phenomenon, while the other is its irreversability. He seems to convey the meaning that one cannot go back to the original position once it has been passed. The original vessel cannot be re-made, which is 'the logic of the concrete', in action, expressed in 'aesthetic' imagery. He is no more irrational than a poet who also uses imagery to express his meaning or perception. The meaning conveyed by means of imagery by the primitve philosopher seems to be akin to momentariness or the *pratityasamutpada* of Buddhist theology. The vessel was, and is no more, and hence the two images are related.

The unconscious motivation is applicable as much to the individual as to the whole community or society or to the whole of humanity sharing complexes of universal import. The need to descend into this dark subterranean region is to capture symbols to express feelings which is universal trait of all humanity, the primitive and the civilised. The primitive philosopher thinks in terms of symbols which by themselves are often surrealistic in nature, that can only be interpreted on several levels in their various ratifications.

Let us refer to another of primitive man's obsession, i.e. the myth of creation. Like death, creation of the universe, the stars, the sun and the moon has been the primitive man's quest as is with his civilised counterpart. The conception of a creator god and creation does occur among heathen forebears such as Tasmanian, the Bushman, the Samang of Mallay Peninsula. Again, we come back to the Adis of Arunachal Pradesh for their myth of creation. According to them in the beginning, there was no shape or form; everything was enveloped in darkness. The myth of creation portrayed in the Bible, and in the Hindu mythology are similar in conception depicts chaos and confusion in the beginning. Their (Adis') story goes like this:

"In the beginning, there was no shape or form but only darkness everywhere. Melo (earth) and Sedi (Sky) lay close together and not far apart as now. Out of their union, things were born; light emerged and landscape as we behold it today with mountains, land and water and all life came into being."

Of course, we immediately come closer to the evolutionist Tylor's conception that while looking at the universe animistically, primitive man endowed the elements, the animals, the plants, and the rocks with personalities and souls. Such beliefs survived into modern civilization among the unlettered lower classes and formed a crust of folklore. In the same vein, some scholars observe that, to the Adis, all existence is endowed with life and the evolution of what we consider inanimate, must have also come through the normal physiological process of birth.

Thus, we are not far removed from the Rig Vedic idea of *Dyaya Prithvi* (the Heaven and Earth) who were together in the beginning of creation, and gave birth to all beings.

The emergence of the world, the sky and earth, the heavenly bodies offer the glimpse of Miltonic grandeur of conception. The way of anthropomorphising the natural courses by the primitive philosopher bears testimony to some psychological compulsion to thus conceptualise the creation. The Vedic lore also tells us that *Hiranyagarbh* laid an egg, one half of which became the sky, while the other half the earth. In Greek mythology two gigantic eggs shining like gold were imagined to have been randomly going round and round and lastly they collided from which emerged the earth and her husband, the sky, and from their union were born all things on earth. The Akash of Arunachal Pradesh is very near to the cosmic egg conception of the origin. While the sky-father conception is found among the ancient Greeks as *Zeus-Pater* who is no other than the Vedic *Dyus-Pitar,* the Konyak Nagas are known to have been practising the cult of the Sky God which they call in their language Gawang. It means literally 'Earth-Sky'. To Kanyak Nagas, the name Gawang denoted not the spiritual essence of the universe but a deity of highly personal character associated with the sky more than the earth.

Among the Polynesian group of Islands, in the mythologies of Hawaii, the Society Island and Tihiti, we come across similar archetypal imagery recurring through the story of Tangaloa (the God of Heaven). A grand idea, proto-type of which can be traced in Vedic script, from the myths of Arunachal Pradesh is a premordial being sacrificing itself so that its body was transferred into different parts of the earth, valleys, mountains and living creatures. This idea reverberates in the famous *Purush-Sukta* in the Rig Veda offering a macro-cosmic idea of the world as a vast personage. The Apa Tanis of Arunachal Pradesh tell the story that all human beings originally clung to the body of the giantess *Kujum Chantu* who died of her own accord, so that they would not fall off and be killed. 'Every part of her body became part of the world and her eyes turned into the Sun and the Moon.' Atharva Veda describes earth as the seat of the highest Brahman, the air his belly, the sky his head, the Sun and the Moon his eyes, fire his mouth and the wind his breathing. The same *Purush* was identified with the creator *Prajapati.* In the mythology of the Adis, as seen earlier, *Doini-Pollo* (the Sun-Moon God) is described as 'the eyes of the world'. The immanence of the creator in the creation itself is a theme of *Upanishads* too.

What is important is not the story, but the whole imagery which is unconscious and symbolical marking the beginning of self-awareness in the primitive philosopher. The spectrum of myths taken literally is worthless, but the symbolism underlining it shows the thinking process of early man which gains primary importance.

MYTHOLOGICAL AND MORPHOLOGICAL INTERPRETATION

Now, we shall turn to mythological, traditional and morphological significance in this study of the two names viz., 'Tiwa' and 'Lalung' of a tribe of North East of India and the folklore connected with them. Interestingly enough, these two names are used simultaneously to identify the same tribe. The Tiwas, also known as Lalungs, have vast treasures of oral literature comprising myths, tales, legends, proverbs, songs and riddles. And, they have played vital role in moulding Assamese social strata and cultural fabrics. This tribe, inhabiting north-eastern slopes of Khasi Hills of Kamrup and Nowgong districts, forms a separate ethnic group within the Bodo branch of the Indo-Mongloid stocks designated as Lalungs in authentic monographs, while scholars and researchers widely recognise them as Tiwas without discarding their other documentary identity.

A legend runs that the Karbis (Mikirs) rescued the Lalungs while Burmese invasion had driven them out of their original habitat in Upper Assam towards the river Kolong in Nowgong district. The Karbis labelled them as 'Lalung' (*Lang* means water, and '*Lung*' means to sink in water) so as to precisely distinguish themselves from that fugitive tribe, living as their neighbours so long. Another version of the legend reads that some clans of the tribe abandoned their original abode of Jaintia Kingdom during factional differences over crowning their chieftain. According to a third version, this tribe deserted Jaintia Hill terrain for practices of immolation of human beings and while crossing the Kapili river, the Karbis helped them, thence calling them Lalung, the people who sank in water.

A traditional narrative depicts the tribe as experts in elephant trapping, forcing them to evince their fall into a deep ditch called *Long* and utilising a long pole called *Lang* in their language. Subsequently, from the conjunction of these two words *Long* and *Lang*, the tribe is believed to have become known as Lalungs.

According to another myth, the original language of this tribe was Sanskrit and they being Kshatriyas—the Hindu caste of warriors and kings—hid in 'Lalung Hills' on north bank of Brahmaputra to escape the wrath of Parshuram who set out to wipe out Kshatriyas to avenge his father's death at the hands of Sahastrabahu Arjun. They gave up speaking Sanskrit and discarded sacred threads from their persons. Their sojourn in the hideouts prolonged for centuries, as a result the race suffered amnesia of its original traditions and tongue. On return to their homeland, they were recognised as Kshatriyas, but were called Lalungs due to their home—Lalung Hills. Medieval period witnessed this attribute while non-Aryan tribes developed tendency to rise to an equal status with the Aryans through 'Sanskritisation process.'

However, a different legend throws light on Mahadev having five mouths (conception of five mouths of Mahadev is a peculiarity among Lalungs) out of which was rolling down *Lal* (drool) during his deep sleep. Mahadev expressed his desire to his consort Parvati to create five human beings, and be wedded with five females being created by Parvati. Those five couples were said to be the first Lalungs on earth and the tribe is named as such, as they are said to have been born from the drool called *Lal*. Thus, they consider and worship Mahadev as their father and supreme God.

Still another myth runs thus : a God *Lungla* was born from Shiva. *Lungla* is a combination of two Lalung words—*Lung* (meaning oozing out of a kind of juice from Shiva), and *La* (meaning five kinds of elements for creating human being, i.e. juice, blood, soil, water and air). The God Lungla married Jayanti Devi, the daughter of Bhagwati, the wife of Shiva. Out of their conjugation were born three daughters Lai, Halali and Lali. The Mikirs are the offsprings of the eldest Lai, the Bodos are believed to be born of Hilali and Lalungs from Lali. Their names and references are frequently found in the Lalung folk songs, three stanza of which are quoted here:

Lali Hilali Lai
dakai patharate ghurailai phurale
ajala lalungak pai .....

The Assamese piece says that Lali, Hilali, and Lai are three sisters. The innocent Lalungs are dragged hither and thither in the low lands ('innocent' in the sense, they were born not due to their fault; and 'dragged hither and thither' means though they were born and descended from such ethereal beings, they are subjected to such cruel conditions).

A myth proclaims that the king of demons Bali, after embracing religion ordained the subjects to accept his religious doctrines. The defaulters were banished with red-marks inscribed upon their foreheads. The persons with the red (*Lal*) marks are ultimately said to have derived their name from the word *Lal* and are known as Lalungs.

A section of their compatriots (Lalungs') shifted to the plains and preferred to be called as 'Tiwas'—a word of their native language which is said to be a combination of two Tiwa words, *Ti* (water) and *Pha* (father); it means the descendants of the water-god. Traditional accounts and mythologies also reveal that these tribals remained in constant association with water, always seeking proximity and settlement near the banks of rivers.

Their myth is related thus : Once the Tiwas prayed to Shiva for the boon to have their king. Having been pleased, Shiva came down to their place of worship and sighted two birds engaged in copulation (*Kamkeli*) in a lake. Out of excitement and passionate desire, at the sight he was so inflamed that he discharged his semen. The discharge fell into a triangular lake nearby. A fish co-incidentally swallowed the semen which formed a human being in its belly. Later, the human body was brought out ripping the belly of the fish (a species known as 'Mali fish') and was nurtured. He was crowned as the first king of the Lalungs. His name is believed to be Malaiali and his progeny used to attach 'ali' as a suffix to their names to identify themselves as the royal breeds. (But 'ali' is also usually used as the suffix to denote the female lineage of a clan in the Lalung society with reference to twelve sisters.) Some clans of the tribe trace their origin totemistically from the stone, tiger and monkey; and, they have peculiar superstitions, beliefs and customs as regards stones, fish and these two animals.

An Angami Naga folktale says that man, tiger and spirit were brothers and were born from the same woman, while Ao Naga tradition states that their ancestors came out of the earth from six stones, i.e. lungterok—*lung* means stone, and *terok* means six—of Chungliyimti village, which is now a Sangtam village on the right bank of river Dikhu opposite to Longsa village. The similarity of these legends of origin can be traced.

According to a traditional narration, 'Tiopha' is the father of the Tiwas. 'Tiopha' might have been compounded from *ti* and *pha* or *pa* (which means the water god). The tribe used to call themselves 'Tiwas' (*ti* means water, *wa* means bank and *sa* means son, i.e. the son of water-god). The Tiperas, a branch of Tibbeto-Burman Mongoloid stock, living at present in Tripura, still call themselves 'Tipra' or 'Tifra', and they are believed to be an offshoot of the Tiwas, having left their original abode, the Tribega kingdom in the Kapili valley, founded around 1900 B.C. It is conjectured that in the ancient times, Tiwas might have been known as Tipra or Tiphra or Tibra and their name might have been changed to Tiwa in due course of time.

Sometimes Tiwas also identify themselves as 'Tiwa Libing' or 'Tiwa-Libung', which, according to their implication, means a superior or civilised man since '*Tiwa*' means 'son of water or river' and 'Ling' means to go. 'Tiwaling' aptly applies to those nomads who roam about from place to place having settlements on the river-banks. 'Tiwaling' might have been conveniently shortened to 'Tiwa''

In Tiwa language, a long river is called 'Loowati' or 'Loowatilung' (wherefrom the word 'luit', another name for the river Brahmaputra, is said to have been derived). Here, '*loowa*' means long, *ti* means water and *tilung* means river. Hence, the possibility of the word Tiwa having been derived from 'Loowatilung' cannot be overlooked.

The interpretation bears testimony to the racial nodes, its migrational imports in moulding the course of folklife, tribal mindset and fixation, its primeval imaginative genius, its beliefs and cults, and aspirations to be transformed into civilised society, unfolding its collective socio-genetic, socio-psychic and cultural patterns which carry significant intrigue for its further scientific investigation.

References

1. **Levi-Straus,** Claude Structural Anthropology, Vol.2, **Penguin, 1973.**
2. **Verrier, Elwin, Myths** of North East Frontier of India, **Shillong , NEFA,** 1958.

3. ——-A Philosophy for NEFA, Shillong, NEFA, 1957.
4. ——-A New Book of Tribal Fiction, Shillong; NEFA, 1970.
5. ——-India's North-East Frontier in the Nineteenth Century, New York ; Oxford Univ. Press, 1959.
6. Nigam, R.C., Abors and Myths of Their Origin, March of India, Vol. VI, 1953.
7. Ering, Oshong, Some Adi Myths, NEFA Information, March, 1965.
8. Furer - Haimendorf -Christoph Von, Apatanis and their Neighbours, London, Routledge, 1962.
9. ——-'Religious Beliefs and Ritual Practices of the Minyong Abors of Assam, India', Anthropos VI, 49, 1954.
10. Roy, Sachin, Aspects of Padam-Minyong Culture, Shillong, NEFA, 1966.
11. Nath, R.M., Background of Assamese Culture, Gauhati, 1978.
12. Upadhyay, Krishnadev and Sen Gupta, Sankar, Studies in Indian Folk Culture, Calcutta; Indian Publication, 1963.
13. Goswami, P.D., Adi Tales, Man I, XXIX, 1949.
14. ———Folk Literature of Assam, University of Gauhati, 1954.
15. Sapir, E., Culture, Languages and Personality - Selected Essays, 1957.
16. Hastings, James (Ed.), Encyclopaedia of Religion and Ethics, Vol-5, New York, 1971–1973.
17. Winternitz, M., A History of Indian Literature, Vol-1 & 2, 1927, 1933. Re-print, New York, Russell and Russell, 1972.
18. Chaudhury, J.N., A Comparative Study of Adi Religion, 1971.
19. Norbeck, Edward, Religion in Primitive Society, 1961.
20. Griffith, R.T.H., The Hymns of the Rig Veda, Benaras, 1926.
21. Lessa, William A. and Evon Z. Vogt, Reader in Comparative Religion - An Anthropological Approach, 1958.

22. Macdonell, A.A. and A.K. Keith, Vedic Index of Names and Subjects, Vol. 1 & 2, 1912.
23. Macdonell, A.A., A Vedic Reader for Students, 1960.
24. Fobbes, C.J.F.S., On Tibeto-Burman Language, J.R.A.S.G.B.I. N.S. Vol. 10, 1878.
25. Lorrain, J.H., A Dictionary of the Abor-Miri Language with Illustrative Sentences and Notes, Shillong, 1910.
26. Shyam Choudhury, N.K. and M.M. Das, The Lalung Society, Calcutta, 1973.
27. Srivastav, L.R.N., The Gallongs, Shillong, Research Deptt., Advisers' Secretariat, 1962.

Chapter 4

Folklore as Critique Culture

STRUCTURAL ANALYSIS

The folklore lays down maxims and constitutes instruments to control the society, provides ideals to be inculcated amongst its members for individual's well-being as well as the general welfare of the community. Folktales have a remarkable capacity for acculturation, assimilation, adjustment and conservation, and at the same time to support the institutions and behaviour patterns of a culture. Besides suggesting rules for conduct, folklore also drives home the need for holding up to scorn those who depart from socially accepted norms, and eulogizing those who follow them, exemplifying the standard-bearers of values and goals of the community. Apart from its didactic function as the charter for belief, model for action, etc., folklore serves as a critique of the socio-cultural mores of the sections of society of which it is an ethnopoetic documentation—that is, folklore being a collective creativity of a collective psyche, its essential function is to be self-reflective, to be critically realistic. Thus, the folklore also provides instruments for socio-cultural protests or criticism. Some folklorists from east European countries and Soviet Union have even gone to the extent of saying that folklore arises from the people, the folk, is the expression of protest and outrage against the exploiting nobles and landowners. Hence, in the Soviet Union folk bards and story-tellers are honoured along with novelists and poets. In Socialist countries of the twentieth century, the governments have taken a part in the process of regulating conformity by awarding prizes to folk poets and folk narrators who attack bourgeois and capitalist villains and extol peasants and Socialist heroes.

In Assamese folk literature also, a few tales which are ribalds (*risques)* meant for cutting jokes-jests that is very hilarious and has a dig at Brahminical (Gosain) orthodoxy, Satras or Vaishnavite (Bhakats) institutions, hypocrisy are available which would substantiate my argument that the views held by some of our scholars that such critical feed-back to our culture is not stressed in our land is absolutely incorrect.

Here, I wish to demonstrate a discourse with a general literary analytic frame-work to drive home the critical point of folktale about the milieu of its origin. The tale is in Angami Naga dramatised and broadcast over AIR Kohima in 1981.

Free rendering in English translation of the tale (in present tense) is given below:

THE STORY OF MEHOVIU

1. Morusa is a dweller of Kidima (a southern Angami village about 10 k.m. from the State Capital Kohima).
2. He is robust health-wise (or has a proportionate physique) and is affluent.
3. After all, he is a good warrior.
4. Morusa thinks of taking a dive into wedlock.
5. But there's no girl in Kidima who could be a match for him.
6. His female relatives gather news about the eligible damsels in the neighbouring villages, and on search, they learn that there's a pretty girl called Mehoviu in the adjoining village.
7. Mehoviu does not know Morusa.
8. But she has heard of him.

9. Actually, she has been dreaming and weaving fantasies of merry making that she eats and drinks at Morusa's house.
10. Representatives are sent to Mehoviu and her consent is obtained.
11. Then, the date on which Mehoviu would arrive to Morusa's house is fixed, and word sent around (accordingly).
12. On the appointed day, Morusa rises early in the morning and chuckling, tells himself:
13. "Tonight, my wife will come.
14. "I must, therefore, go for head-hunting and come with a head (trophy).
15. "In the evening, when my bride comes, we would be all feasting RUPIE" (the ceremonial meat served in the feast to celebrate a head-hunting success).
16. He togs up and goes for head-hunting.
17. But he finds no warriors.
18. When he is passing by a village, he comes across a plump belle.
19. Morusa does not want to slay a girl (balks).
20. Nevertheless, he kills her and chops her head off for want of warriors (men).
21. He brings the head home, and in the twilight, they are relishing feast around the head and waiting for the bride's arrival.
22. They wait and wait, but Mehoviu does not appear.
23. Wondering as to what has happened, folks conjecture that Morusa has been jilted.
24. Then reaches the news that when Mehoviu was about to leave, a head-hunter slew her.
25. (It's not long before) it dawns on Morusa that he has killed his own wife-to-be and has carried the head home.
26. Morusa is distressed.

The tale of Mehoviu is a well crafted short story, with its tense thematic progression. Its focal action is on inadvertent killing of his own prospective bride by a capricious youth. The exposition of the story with the first three sentences delineating the male protagonist's physical nature along with his personal traits of bellicose character and abundant riches, in a few pen-strokes, takes off with a complex sentence (Sent.4) establishing romantic mood of his mental life to plunge into nuptial bond; thereafter, triggers the action of the story with the disjunctive sentence (Sent.5) which poses a problem. Here, the non-availability of a suitable match (nubile) is counter-poised by the non-availability of a warrior (man) outside the village; since no cultural proscription of female head-hunting is available, the plot renders Morusa to cut short the dreams not only of his fiancee, but his own, killing Mehoviu, the female protagonist and none else. The contrivance provides fatality for both, Mehoviu and Morusa (as the perfect match is wiped out at his own hands). Therefore, the tale is a powerful tragedy.

The sentence-6 has a systolic poise as the problem so identified is nearing to be solved which is subsequently solved. With the background information furnished in three sentence-paragraphs (Sent's 7,8 and 9 which serve double functions of providing mental and emotional gamut of the girl, unconsciously pining and longing for Morusa, and the strangeness, or, unfamiliarity that pervaded between them that played vital role before and after her consent), the narrative gathers diastolic movement in the collateral paragraph (Sent. 10 to 12). Of course, here the contrivance in the tale of unfamiliarity between the two protagonists appears to have a flaw as regards plausibility since the tribal society is very much permissive so far as the prospective couple is concerned who is soon brought to intimacy or to courtship particularly when their matrimonial cord is finalised. However, the non-availability of the match, as stated earlier, works for the suspension of our disbelief of their strangeness to each other.

The action depicted in sentences 11 to 15 is charged with emotional crescendo, suspense and vivid scenarios shifting rapidly. It has its own anti-thesis since the decision on bride's arrival itself is the source of its reversal and final termination; it is potent enough to throw ripples of excitement in Morusa arousing him to display his chivalry by head-hunting which is in consonance with his bellicose nature. His awakening-arousing with chuckle in the morning, in fact, is apparently physical one and the display of his gallantry (which ultimately proves to be a dastardly act), performance of a ceremonial feast appropriate to the festive mood of the occasion and thereafter, night-copulation (implied) is the natural course of the romantic day, though among tribals it is not customary for the bride-groom to go head-hunting before wedding.

The protagonist's desire, his togging up, setting out and searching for warriors to fight with all these sequences (Sent's 16,17) have picturesque qualities of cinematic shots, and serve neatly prepared foreground for the catastrophic peak-moment whereupon he commits uxoricide (Sent.20) unwittingly through want of identity, and want of warrior-man (Sent.19). Of course, there is no taboo prescribed so far in the cultural milieu proscribing female head-hunt. Therefore, the protagonist's balking and jibbing ("Morusa does not want to slay a girl.") is nothing but suggestive of his dormant humanitarian traits which, however, no longer desist him from his final horrid act, in the face of its cultural sanction. Here, man is stretched to the conformity of the corporate body of society wherein lopping off of the head of any human victim irrespective of the sex, age and status earns the slayer no less prestige than the killing of armed warrior.

The climactic moment has high-pitch dramatic irony and the falling action-reversal (Sent's 21 to 23) shows lull, stasis and prelude to the revelation—unravelling the knot, the denouement—of the ghastly act of butchering his own wife to be by Morusa who is, according to the surmise of the jubilant people celebrating, feasting around her head itself, jilted by the bride due to her non-arrival; while in fact, she was jilted by him most savagely under the cover of a practice culturally motivated and socially supported.

The crux of the tale is the realization of the protagonist—that the woman head-hunted by him and the bride who is eagerly awaited on her non-arrival at the appointed hour by the rejoicing people is the same one that correlates the incident with the arrival of the news (Sent.24) about her being slain.

Head-hunting practice was the cultural norm of the Naga societies. Internecine village-feuds, personal animosity and vengeance had been the motivating force in the initial stage, which became an effective incentive to earn prestige, valour and insignia for a victory of a successful head-hunter; subsequently, it developed into a degenerated, morbid ethos of personal bravery.The feathers in a head-gear worn by the Angami male indicating the number of heads won by him shows the irrational, abominable depth to which the inhuman practice plunged. The present tale makes a mockery of this through its paradoxical situation unfolding the apparent bravery culminating into cowardice and successful hunt-victory into defeat; cowardice, because the hunted creature is his own wife, and defeat, because it has turned into an inexorable personal tragedy. The tale abounds with travesty and ironic juxtapositions, viz. human/inhuman, life/death, bravery/cowardice, success/defeat, rejoice/affliction, material/spiritual, and the apparent/real, etc.

In the physical world surrounding the protagonist with its material (affluence), physique (flesh-sex implied) and violence (head-hunt), the affliction caused to him (Sent.26) due to his personal tragedy of his own making is powerful enough to throw ripples in his consciousness which is suggestive of his real awakening (Sent.25-' it dawns on Morusa ..'). Here, the practice which is safely operative in a cultural cognitive anthropological cosmos is proved to be out of place in a personal cosmos. Inevitably, the perturbance in an individual's consciousness caused by a pervert social-practice is, in fact, a stir, also a perturbance in the consciousness of other members of the group. The malady emanating from the thought system of the society leading to dead end, could be penetrated by the befitting severe shock-treatment received by the protagonist who is plunged into human pathos (at the open-ended closure of the tale).

The tale is a classic example as critique culture.

Had the protagonist met a warrior when he set out for a hunting spree, and in the ensuing fight if his head lopped off, there would have been no tale to tell since the critical point aimed at would be lost in the wilderness, and the tale would fall flat; the maiden would be in woes and morose for some time and the whole episode would vanish into oblivion. In George Lukacsian sense of critical realism, the present tale, a literary artifact, has achieved what it could - the best by allusion and in an implicit way.

For the structural analysis of folkloristic text considered as the linguistic model, Sahlin has summed up his idea thus: 'What is apparent is false, and what is hidden from perception and contradicts it is true.' Here, the tale contains two-fold apparents—one at the textual-structural level and other at the level of thematic content. Certainly, there are other models of narrative structure analysis which may shed more light on the critical point of the issue. However, the present discussion has made the apparent or manifest content to reveal to us what is hidden behind ; while on the other hand, the protagonist has seen his hunting exercise as 'self-deception' crossing across the thick dark-terrain surrounding his consciousness which is quite in conformity with the jerk—a human trembling at twilight.

References

1. Lukacs, George, The Meaning of Contemporary Realism, London, Merlin Press, 3rd edn., 1972.
2. Hawkes, Terence, Structuralism and Semiotics, London, Methuen, 1977.
3. Propp, Vladimir J., Morphology of the Folktale, Austin, University of Texas Press, (Original in Russian, 1928), 1968; 2nd edn., Austin, 1970.
4. Dundes, Alan, Structural Typology in North-American Indian Folktales, Dundes (ed.), Indiana University, 1965.
5. Bascom, W.R., Four Functions of Folklore in Alan Dundes

(ed.) The Study of Folklore, New Jersey ; Prentice Hall Inc., Englewood Cliffs, 1965.

6. Culler, Jonathan, Structuralist Poetics : Structuralism, Linguistics and the Study of Literature, London ; Routledge & Kegan Paul, 1975.
7. Harris, Merwin, The Rise of Anthropological Theory, London; Routledge & Kegan Paul, 1972.
8. Grimmes, G.E., The Thread of Discourse, The Hague, Janua Linguaram, 1975.
9. Lazlo, Halasz (ed.), Literary Discourse : Aspects of Cognitive and Social Psychological Approaches, Berlin, 1987.
10. Chatman, Seymour, Story and Discourse, Ithaca and London; Cornell University Press, 6th edn. 1993.

Chapter 5

Folktale on a Taboo

PSYCHOANALYTICAL VIEW

The psychological-psychoanalytic folklorists view the materials of folklore neither aesthetically nor functionally but behaviouristically. This School provides the only non-formalistic theory based on interpretation of folktale using Freudian sexual symbolism. Many writers are of the view that the folklore texts are to be interpreted symbolically in terms of sexual imagery and Oedipus Complex.

Infantile and half forgotten or repressed sexual drives are transformed by certain mechanism into symbols represented by objects and images of daily life. Since the dream is equated by them as the myths of individuals, the same mechanism for interpretation of dreams—dream symbols, could be applied to myths and folktales. C.G. Jung substituted social unconsciousness for the symbolism of sexual urges. On the assumption of dream as individual myth, and myth as social dream, the myths reveal the psychic repression of the childhood of a whole race or culture. Some folklorists modified their findings or undertook fresh researches basing on Jung's findings of 'Collective Unconsciousness' and personal unconsciousness.

As pointed out by Merwin Harris, the "Freud's system could only generate the universals of culture and a few crude stages of a unilinear evolution. Specific cultural differences and similarities were beyond his grasp and interest." However, the concept of 'Collective Unconscious' has been widely accepted as a common postulate, as an empirical matter in the field of this discipline. Inspite of several controversies and rejection of psycho-analytical theory and Oedipus Complex by many schools of thought by Boasians, Malinowski, Mead, Benedict etc., some eminent folklorists continue to use their methodology for interpretation of folklore.

My object here is to make some observations on a folktale from Tripura regarding a social taboo-incest, from the psychoanalytical perspective. Of course, it is intended to be in a free vein, rather than strictly equating the objects etc. to stock-symbols. The tale runs thus :

"Two young persons, who happen to be brother and sister went to work in the *jhum* field. Every day while returning home, they used to bathe in a stream. One day, it so happened that the brother saw the naked body of the sister. This aroused sensuous passion in his mind. He decided to marry her. They reached home, but he refused to take meal unless their parents would submit to his demand. All attempts to persuade him to give up such an unsocial demand failed. So, they at last agreed and assured him of making necessary arrangements after harvest. The matter was concealed from the sister. But from a casual remark made by her grandmother at an unguarded moment, she at last came to know the term of the compromise. She at once reacted, ran and climbed up a *Chhatim* tree (*Alstonia Scholaris).* The parents and villagers followed to catch her but failed. Sacrifices to pacify her were made. At last, the adamant brother was also sacrificed. The brother then turned into a Chameleon and chased her. So she requested the tree to stretch itself higher and higher. Thus, she ascended to heaven. While leaving the tree, she broke its head. That is why, it is said, the head of the *Chhatim* tree is flat and Chameleon even today gets angry whenever it faces man, and the lightning is nothing but the private parts of the sister."

The tale is on the violation of a taboo, and the motivation to commit incest with blood-relative i.e. sister, which, in fact, does not succeed and the attempts get frustrated, half way.

There are folktales which fully depict such incestuous episodes. Ruth Benedict (1887-1948) has pointed out that the tribal mythologies narrated violations of taboos, such as the hero-trickster in the 'Journal of American Folklore' sleeping with his mother-in-law, which would never be tolerated in real life. In the 'Rationale of the Dirty Jokes' (1968), Hungarian scholar G.Lengman gives attention to the most current folktale genre of modern society and looks beneath the seemingly obvious motivation of dirty jokes to violate sexual and anal taboos. The general tendencies of the individuals having incestuous phantasies are implied in the Oedipus Complex too.

The present tale states the same problem being faced by a female protagonist whose naked body, while taking bath in the stream, inflamed the sexual passion in her brother. He abandoned taking his meal till such time his desire to marry her is fulfilled by their parents who apparently agree to compromise with the social interdict under compulsion when all their efforts to persuade him to give up such an unsocial demand fail. However, it is only the grandmother, supposed to be the carrier of social maxims to succeeding generations and to be a watchdog of their compliance in the society, who makes casual remark about the compromise that sparks off the incident, and the panic-stricken sister runs amok, climbes up *Chhatim* tree (*Chhatim* means umbrella that protects. The shape of the tree is like an umbrella). Persuasion and sacrifices are made by her parents and villagers to appease her to return , but to no avail, and in the course the brother is also sacrificed. His sacrifice, rather we may call it as his repressed carnal desire, is transformed and it takes the physical shape of a Chameleon. (only the Chameleon can run so fast on the tree) to catch the girl. The functional meaning of this kind of lizard to be known is to understand the mythological setting— its context in the tale. In order to suit the surroundings, the Chameleon is able to change its colours to conceal itself, which is its defence-mechanism. The sexual passion wears such masks of changing colours for its concealment and indulgence in deception. Therefore, the Chameleon chasing the girl on the tree represents the trickster-hero in the transformed form, and stands as a phallic figure, say a phallus itself).

Out of fright, the female protagonist makes a bid to escape–a flight, requesting the tree to stretch itself higher and higher. (Conversely, the tree-trunk is the abode of the Chameleon and serves as its replica–full of growth, virility and erection. It is noteworthy here that in Ao Naga folktale, 'Girl with Tree as Husband', a girl marries the tree.) Ironically, the female protagonist of the tale under discussion takes shelter atop the tree to escape and her entreaty for its elongation made unaware of the conceit lying beneath is conceded to. However, while leaving the tree for her ultimate flight into the sky, she breaks its head to cut short the chase by Chameleon which is an act of castration resulting into its permanent atrophy (flat head) and in the same sense, diminutive shape of the Chameleon, its replica.

The incestuous instinct always causes fear and evokes unconscious guilt later, but the intruders and irritants in its designs are looked at with frown. The Chameleon's anger as attributed and imput to it in the tale is quite obvious. It is a rhetorical step from here to envision the lurking Chameleon now sitting on the top of the tree with eternally burning passionate thirst and looking beyond vacantly into the sky, wherein the female protagonist has disappeared. (The ascent of the girl into heaven signifies the divinity that she attained which juxtaposes the lewd with the divine.) The fear is one of the primitive, violent, and usually crippling emotions marked by extensive bodily changes, and by behaviour of the flight or concealment character. The genital of the female protagonist turning into lightning is of tremendous fascination, but of a fierceful and disastrous character, and that being so, it stands as a primordial image of cosmic phenomenon. Nevertheless, its symbolic meaning of love usually found in the dream - mechanism can be assigned to it—the love, which if violated, invites death and destruction.

The tale has anthropomorphic and animistic elements which are woven together along with thematic content of social taboo. Even though, the aetiological purpose echoes in the tale, the phantastic primitive mind with grand imagination cannot be overlooked. The didactic tone of looking at the violation of the social taboo as bringing disorder in the natural course of life and consequently the incest as a stigma— like the lowest lizard, a mean loathful creeping creature—is perfectly under play in the tale. The manifestation of the thematic content is quite in consonance with the social thought system of our modern civilization, as of to-day.

References

1. Dorson, Richard M., Introduction to Folklore and Folklife; An Introduction, Chicago; Chicago Univ. Press, 1972.
2. Harris, Merwin, The Rise of Anthropological Theory, London ; Routledge & Kegan Paul, 1972.
3. Freud, Sigmund, Jokes and Their Relation to the Unconscious, London, Hogarth Press, 1960.
4. ——Totem and Taboo, London, 1950.
5. ——Interpretation of Dreams, Vol. 4, Penguin, 1976.
6. ——The Occurrence in Dreams of Material from Fairy Tales, Standard Ed., 12, 281, 1913.
7. ——withOppenheim, D.E., Dreams in Folklore; New York, Part - I, Standard Ed., 12, 177, 1958.
8. Jastrov, Joseph, Freud : His Dream and Sex Theories, New York; Simon & Sechuster, Inc., 1969.
9. Jung, C.G., 'The Concept of the Collective Unconscious' (1936), 'The Phenomenology of the Spirit in Fairy Tales" (1945/1948), and 'On the Psychology of the Trickster- Figure' (1954), in Collected works, Vol. IX, London, Routledge & Kegan Paul, 1948-55.

Chapter 6

Ritual

Ritual, pervasive kind of behaviour, can be seen as basic to the understanding of man. Man is sometimes described or defined as a basically rational, economic, political or playing species. Man may, however, also be viewed as a ritual being, who exihibits a striking parallel between his ritual and verbal behaviour. Since ritual is a specific, observable kind of behaviour based upon established or traditional rules, laid down by all known societies, it is possible to view ritual as a way of defining or describing man.

Just as language is a symbolic system based upon arbitrary rules, rituals may be viewed as a symbolic system of acts based upon arbitrary rules. The intricate, yet complex, relation between ritual and language can be seen in the history of various attempts to explain ritual behaviour. In most explanations, language becomes a necessary factor concerning the nature of ritual, and the specific form of language that is tied to explanations of ritual is the language of myth. Both myth and ritual remain fundamental to any analysis of religions.

As regards the nature and origin of ritual, we have three general approaches to its understanding. It was by means of historical origin, that an attempt was earlier made to explain ritual as well as religion. The attempt largely assumed an evolutionary hypothesis that would explain the development of ritual behaviour through history. In order to explain the universal scope of ritual, scholars had to depend upon the success in locating the oldest cultures and cults. The idea was to discover this origin to enable them to further explain the contemporary rituals of man.

The use of primitive cultures and primitive religion comes from this approach in seeking an answer to the meaning of ritual, myth, and religion. In this, the main topic for speculation was the sacrifice of either men or animals. The exact motivation or cause of such sacrificial ritual, as shown by W. Robertson-Smith, a British scholar, seemed to be the need for communion between members of a primitive group and their God. The origin of ritual, therefore, was supposed to have been traced in totemic (animal symbolic clan) cults, and the totemism was believed to be the earliest stage of religion and ritual. We find several secondary stages of development of this original sacrificial ritual.

The influence of Smith's ideas can be widely traced in Sigmund Freud, the father of Psychoanalysis, Sir James Frazer, English anthropologist and Emile, French Sociologist. Here, the scholars found the division of experience into the Sacred and Profane. They held that the ritual behaviour entails an attitude concerned with the sacred; and sacred acts and things are symbolic representation of society. In his *Moses and Monotheism*, Freud has shown that the origin of religion and ritual is to be found in sacrifice. However, the origin - evolutionary hypothesis of ritual behaviour was rejected by the leading contemporary scholars on the ground that it was nothing but theoretical notions and creative speculations falling short of explaining human behaviour that they cannot be confirmed or denied. It was the functional approach which emphasised the empirical data collected by actual observation. The nature of ritual, in other words, is to be defined in terms of its function in a society, which means the ritual behaviour is here explained in terms of individual needs and social equilibrium. Ritual is thus viewed as an adaptive and adjustive response to the social and physical environment; many leading contemporary authorities have adopted this approach as the adequate way to explain ritual, myth and religion.

From a logical point of view, functionalism remains a heuristic device (or indicator), for describing the role of ritual in society. If it is asserted that a society functions adequately only if necessary needs are satisfied; and it is further asserted that ritual does satisfy that need, scholars have not been able to conclude that; therefore, ritual is present in that society without committing logical fallacy of affirming the consequent. To assert that the need is satisfied "if and only if" ritual is present is a tautology and a reversal of the claim to be empirical.

Most historians of religions, such as Rudolf Otto in Germany, Mircea Eliade in the United States, and E.O. James in England, while rejecting both the above approaches to an adequate explanation of ritual, held the view that ritual behaviour signifies or expresses the sacred (the realm of transcendent or ultimate reality). Their approach to the study of ritual is centred on the studies of historians of religions. However, it has never been represented as an explanation of ritual. The problem with it remains that it cannot be confirmed unless scholars agree beforehand that such a transcendent reality exists.

In the study of ritual behaviour, the terms sacred (the transcendent realm) and profane (the realm of time, space, and cause and effect) have remained useful in distinguishing it from other types of actions. Of course, we do not find an exact definition of these terms in the study of ritual, scholars are agreeable to the main characteristics of these two terms. According to Durkheim, the French Sociologist, ritual is a determined mode of action. The reference, or object, of ritual is the belief system of a society, which is constituted by a classification of everything into the two realms of the sacred and the profane. It is taken as a universal feature of religion. Belief systems, myths, and the like, are viewed as expressions of the nature of the sacred realm in which ritual becomes the determined conduct of the individual in a society expressing a relation to the sacred and the profane. The sacred is that aspect of a community's beliefs, myths, and sacred objects that is set apart and forbidden. The function of ritual in the community is that of providing proper rules for action in the realm of the sacred as well as providing a bridge for passing into the realm of the profane.

This dichotomy is represented in infinite variations not only between cultures, but also within a culture. What is holy for a sacred King, Priest, or Shaman (or religious personage having healing and psychic transformation powers), for example, will differ from the proper ritual of others in the community who are related to them, even though they share the same belief systems. The main feature that sustains their relations as well as sets their limits is the ritual of initiation.

Beyond this dichotomy of sacred and profane thought and action, a feeling or emotion of respect, awe, fascination, or dread in relation to the sacred can be shown as the main characteristic of ritual action; while the other characteristics of ritual involve its dependence on a belief system usually expressed in the language of myth, and one that is symbolic in relation to its reference.

The function of ritual depends upon its reference. Ritual is quite often described as a symbolic expression of actual social relations, status, or the role of individual in a society. Ritual is also described as referring to a transcendent, numinous (spiritual) reality and the ultimate values of a community. Ritual as symbolic behaviour presupposes that the action is nonrational whatsoever its referent. It means, the means-end relation of ritual to its referent is not intrinsic or necessary. The basic problem in all of this is that ritual is described from an observer's point of view . Whether ritual man is basically nonrational or rational, as far as his behaviour and his belief system are concerned, it is wholly dependent upon whether he also understands both his behaviour and belief to be symbolic of social, psychological, or numinous realities. The notion of the sacred as a transcendent reality may, however, come closest to the participant's own experience. The universal nature of the sacred-profane dichotomy remains a disputed issue.

The ritual will remain a mystery until such time the flaw

in functional description of ritual and belief is overcome. However, the progress made in the study of language may be of immense help in devising a more adequate explanation of non-verbal behaviour in general and of ritual in particular.

All rituals are dependent upon some belief system for their complete meaning. A great many rituals are patterned after myths. Such rituals can be typed as imitative rituals, which means the ritual repeats the myth or an aspect of the myth. In a passage from an Indian Brahmana (a Hindu Scripture) the answer to the question of why the ritual is performed is that the gods did it this way "in the beginning." Another best example is the rituals of New Year, which very often repeat the story of creation, which can be seen as a repetition of the creative act of the gods, a return to the beginning. It can be discerned that all rituals repeat myths or basic motifs in myths. In other words, myths are the librettos for rituals. Nevertheless, some rituals do repeat the story of myth and represent an important type of ritual behaviour, even though the type cannot be universalized as a description of all ritual action.

We can classify rituals into positive or negative rituals. While most posititive rituals are linked with consecrating or renewing an object or an individual, negative rituals are always in relation to positive rituals behaviour. Avoidance is a term that better describes the negative ritual; the Polynesian word *tabu* (English taboo) is a popular descriptive term for this kind of ritual. This term is applied to those rituals that link something to be avoided or forbidden. Hence, negative rituals focus on rules of prohibition, which encompass infinite variety of rites and behaviour. The common characteristic of all can be seen in breaking of the ritual rule which brings in a dramatic change, usually some misfortune in ritual man. However, variation in this type should be noted from within a culture or cross-culturally. What is prohibited for a subject; for example, may not be prohibited for a king, chief, or a shaman. Contact with the forbidden or transgression of the ritual rules is often atoned by rituals of purification.

The sacrificial rituals are very complex and diverse throughout the world. The significance of this type is well documented in the history of religions, as it has been seen as the earliest or elementary form of religion itself. Its distinctive feature is to be found in the destruction, either partly or totally, of the victim. The victim need not be human or animal; vegetables, cakes, milk, eggs and the like are also "victims" in this type of ritual. The total or partial destruction may take place through burning, dismembering or cutting into pieces, eating or burying. The sacrificial rituals fall into two classes : those in which the participant or participants receive the benefits of the sacrificial act and those in which an object is the direct recipient of the action. This highlights the fact that not only the individuals are affected by sacrificial ritual but also objects such as houses, a particular place, a thing, an action (such as a hunt or war), a family or community, or spirits or gods that become the intended recipients of the sacrifice.

Rituals of passage have often been described as rituals that can be found in practically all religious traditions, identified by the basic characterstic of the life-crisis, transition from one mode of life to another. These rituals mark a crisis in individual or community life. Generally, they often define the life of an individual. They include rituals of birth , puberty (entrance into the full social life of a community), marriage, conception, and death. Many of these rituals mark a separation from an old situation or mode of life, a transition rite celebrating the new situation, and a ritual of incorporation. Rituals of initiation into a secret society or a religious vocation (viz, priesthood, ascetic life, medicine man) are often included among rites of passage as characteristic rituals of transition. One of the dominant motifs of these rituals is the emphasis on separation, as either a death or a return to infancy, or the womb. In southern India, a striking example is the Hindu rite of being "twice born". The young boy who receives the sacred thread in the *Upanayana* ritual, a ceremony of initiation, goes through an elaborate ritual that is seen as a second birth.

Rituals such as Baptism in early Christianity, Yoga in certain parts of India, and the complex puberty rituals among North American Indian cultures exemplify this motif of death and rebirth in rites of passage.

From Mircea Eliade's point of view, initiation rituals are to be interpreted both historically and existentially. They are related to the history and structure of a particular society and to an experience of the sacred that is both trans-historical and transcendent of a particular social or cultural context. Culture, from this perspective, can be viewed as a series of cults, or rituals, that transform natural experiences into cultural modes of life. This transformation involves both the transmission of social structures and the disclosure of the sacred and spiritual life of man.

All the patterns, emphasized by Eliade, include a separation or symbolic death, followed by a rebirth. They include rites all the way from separation from the mother to the more complex and dramatic rituals of circumcision, ordeals of suffering, or a descent into hell, all of which are symbolic of a death followed by a rebirth. Rites of withdrawal and quest, as well as ritual characteristics of shamans and religious specialists, are typically initiatory in theme and structure. Some of the most dramatic rituals of this type express a death and return to a new period of gestation and birth, often in terms that are specifically embryological. Lastly, there are the actual rituals of physical death itself, a rite of passage and transition into a spiritual or immortal existence.

There is a striking contrast in the use of all these typologies to interpret the meaning of ritual. This contrast can be described in terms of two positions: the first emphasizes the socio-psychological function of ritual; the second asserts the religious value of ritual—a specific expression of a transcendental reality.

Ritual behaviour is obviously a means of nonverbal communication and meaning. Thus, the meaning of ritual is often looked for in the verbal, spoken word or a belief system that is taken as its semantic correlate. The spoken elements in a ritual setting do often reveal the meaning of a ritual by reference to a belief system or mythology, but not always. Such a connection has led to an overemphasis on the importance of the belief system or myth over ritual. To assert that myths disclose more than ritual ever can is an oversimplification of the complex correlation of these two important aspects of religion. Theories about rituals are either deduced from the primary literature of a religious tradition or are translated into written language as a result of observation.

Ritual can be studied as a nonverbal communication disclosing its own structure and semantics. Scholars have only recently turned to a systematic analysis of this important aspect of human behaviour; and progress in kinesics, the study of nonverbal communication, may furnish new approaches to the analysis of ritual. This development may well parallel the progress in linguistics and facilitate the analysis of myth as an aspect of language.

A complete analysis of ritual would also include its relation to art, architecture and particular objects used in ritual such as specific forms of ritual dress. All of these components are found in ritual contexts, and all of them are non verbal in structure and meaning.

Most rituals mark off a particular time of the day, month, year, stage in life, or commencement of a new event or vocation. This temporal characteristic of ritual is often called "sacred time". Another special aspect of ritual is described as "sacred space". Time and space are essential features of ritual action, and both mark a specific orientation or setting for ritual. Examples of ritual time and ritual space orientation can be found in the rituals for building the sacrifice in Brahmanic Indian ritual texts; for the building of a Hindu temple or a Christian cathedral; and for consecrating those structures that symbolise a definite space-time orientation in which rituals are enacted. The shape, spatial orientation and location of the ritual setting are essential features of the semantics of ritual action.

When particular ritual objects, dances, gestures, music and dress are included in the study of ritual, the total structure and meaning of ritual behaviour far exceed any one description or explanation of ritual man.

Though the term ritual has often been used to describe the determined, or fixed, behaviour of both animals and men, the future study of ritual may disclose that this behaviour, found throughout history and cultures, is as unique to man as his capacity for speaking language, and that change in ritual behaviour is parallel to, or correlated with, change in language. Although great progress has been made in the analysis of man as the species who speaks, the syntax and semantics of ritual man are yet to be discovered.

THE DEITY DARAI AND EUNUCH PRIESTHOOD

Now, equipped with full knowledge of ritual, we shall attempt to give treatment to the topic,' deity Darai and eunuch priesthood'. Darai is a female deity of obscure origin. She is worshipped in the contiguous districts of Cachar (Assam) and Sylhet (Bangladesh) by the people of lower strata of the society. The worshipping rituals, one or two, are still to be officiated, as a rule, by eunuch priests.

The eunuch priesthood is not an unusual phenomenon in the history of religion. Quite a large number of ancient societies practised worshipping such celebrated deities under the eunuch priesthood. Of course, it is not a widely diffused institution. However, in certain far-flung remote areas, ramifications of the practice still exist. An outline of its growth and course of transformation of this institution is drawn here.

Darai is worshipped by Sylhetis and Cacharis in the form of image which depicts her as a stark naked deity in blazing red complexion. The deity with four arms holds a snake, a lotus and conch shell in three hands while the fourth hand covers her genital. On the back-arch of her vehicle tortoise, she rests her feet.

Her blazing red complexion and snake denote the fiery

sexual passion; whereas her free hand covering her genital is itself an act of inflaming the dark instincts since the beholder is infatuated to see what is concealed. The symbolic values of snake have undergone changes of cult context through the millennia, but essentially they exert the same psychological power as they have always done. In southern India, women desiring children set up snake-stones (naga-kals), for the snake is a phallic symbol and is also associated with prolific offspring and fertility of the Earth, being termed the 'Kshetra-devata' deity of the fields.

Just as the tree reaches from the ground towards heaven, the lotus plant (one of the words for which is *pankaja*, literally ' born from the mud') grows from darkness in the bed of a river or pool to blossom in the light and air on the surface of the water. In this sense, the lotus is a transition symbol but, unlike the *nagas*, it is not dangerous and is inherently beautiful. The light of the lotus is always auspicious, and it is incorporated in the temple sculpture as part of the profusion of the sacred, primeval forest. It is also represented as the throne of gods and goddesses, whose haloes often assume the shape of the lotus blossom, and is held by several deities of the Jain, Buddhist and Hindu pantheons. Real lotuses are among the principal offerings made to images of these deities; lotus petals may be strewn upon magical and meditational diagrams (*yantras* or *mandalas*), which are drawn in accordance with a pattern based upon the shape of a lotus. It is ubiquitous in Indian art, both as a living expression of the beauty of nature and as a literary or visual metaphor, expressing the radiance of a beautiful woman or the spiritual ascendancy of a god.

The most frequently used Sanskrit word for a lotus is *padma*. Its feminine form, Padma, is another name of the Goddess Lakshmi known throughout India as the embodiment of good fortune and victory. Also known as Shri, meaning 'The Radiant', 'The Glorious', 'Good Fortune', Lakshmi is best known in the Hindu pantheon as the chief wife of God Vishnu, among whose hand-held attributes is the lotus. In early Buddhist sculpture she frequently appears standing upon a lotus, both with water from two pitchers held in the trunks of a pair of flanking elephants; she is, of course, intimately associated with water, the element connected with knowledge and mental power.

The divinity of the most holy river, Ganga, is depicted as a beautiful young woman standing upon an aquatic creature. Often, the Goddess Ganga holds a lotus in one hand, the most beautiful–and symbolically charged–of the water flowers. Vishnu, the Hindu god associated with creation and preservation myths whose various incarnations restore the balance of cosmic forces sustaining the universe, usually carries a conch-shell and a lotus in his hands. Thus, the list is inexhaustive.

The same lotus motif is present in the deity Darai. The conch shell is generally used for blowing purpose at the time of worshipping deities to invoke the powers associated with aquatic elements. Vishnu uses it as a war-horn on the battlefield. It is a sacred instrument in ritual worship. The worship of deity Darai is normally performed preferably on the fifth day of the light half of the moon (Panchami) at midnight hours consecutively for three days. Her worship demands offering of eggs which forms essential part of the ritual. Here, it may be noted that the Dimasas, popularly known as Hill Kacharis, the inhabitants of North Cachar Hills, Karbi Anglong, Cachar and Nowgong districts of Assam and Dhansiri region of Nagaland, consider eggs (*daodi*) as the symbol of creation. After the birth of a child, a Dimasa midwife places an egg on the altar of Sibrai, the most benevolent god of the Dimasas' and praying for the well-being of the child she breaks the egg with a single stroke; the breaking-act is considered to be the beginning of life of the new-born baby. If blood comes out from the egg, the Dimasas consider it ominous for the baby.

While worshipping Darai, one egg is salvaged at the fag-end of each day's puja and all other lots are hurled by the priest from a distance on the sharp edge of a cleaver. If all of them fall on the sharp edge, it is considered to be an ominous sign. The last one besmeared with vermillion is used by the priest for performance of a vanishing trick. Also, tortoise is sacrificed on the occasion of her worship in order to wield and attain complete communion with the goddess Darai; the act also serves to propitiate her for abundance of life.

In fact, the whole ritualistic performance is conducted single handed by her devotee and specially appointed priest, locally called Gurma, who is a eunuch dancer believed to have been privileged, none other than him, to worship Darai. The goddess is considered to be a child giver and normally a barren-childless person having obligation to fulfil a vow or to submit an oblation knocks her doors, but never without the accompaniment of a Gurma to carry out puja rites.

In the foreground of the deity image, the Gurma with his flocks forms a rendezvous and throughout the night the scenic platform is filled with their chorus-song and dance on the rhythm and beats of *Mridanga* (Tabur). The Gurma remains clad in female dancer's attire, holding and waving with both hands a turf-fan (*chamar* made from yak's tail). Gradually, as the night advances and its stillness thickens, the whole temperament of the dancers turns to display voluptuous and seductive postures and eroticism with loud chuckles making their movements rapid and erratic, swinging and flinging their bodies jauntily with jerks and twists, till such time the spectacle reaches the height of suggesting combinations and permutations of sexual activity. Their violent movements, sometimes full of long strides, are followed by songs composed of words of local vulgar vocabulary. One will not find any sort of religious allegory nor any artistic demonstration in this rite. In an overstated but wholly credible display of supple sexuality, half way through the dance turns to filthy and crude gestures of copulation. At such a peak moment of disgusting obscene act, majority of the audience leave the scene . Finally, it is at this climactic juncture, the magical use of the eggs and other such rituals are performed to complete and then to terminate the worship.

Now, let us take a view at the vehicle tortoise on which Darai rides; the tortoise occupies an exalted position in the folklore of many races of Asia and America. In Satapatha Brahaman, Prajapati while producing all creatures, is said to have changed himself into a tortoise. Turtle, the second incarnation of Vishnu, the *brahmans'* god *par excellence* who becomes incarnate in every universal time-cycle, is said to have been involved in the myth of the churning of the cosmic ocean. Here, the god undergoes transformations in order to restore universal harmony. During Gurjara-Pratihara period (8th-9th century), Yamuna, a celebrated river-deity, has been depicted in the sculpture as riding on a turtle. Here, one of the two sacred rivers of northern India is personified as goddess taking her name from the river Jumna. In several cases, the tortoise as a primordial creature, is associated with water-deities or the deities of procreation. It is worshipped by the Kolarians as a river deity. Among certain Red Indian tribes, turtle killing ceremony is performed for availing abundant showers of rain for rich crops. In the islands of Torry Straits, many magical ceremonies, chiefs of a sexual character, were performed to prepare a canoe for turtle fishing. Turtle dances were also performed to ensure success in fishing. The four-armed Japanese creator goddess sits on a tortoise. (Here, the similarity with the goddess Darai is discernible. The outstretched four arms generally represent the extension of space embracing four directions). So also, in north American myths, the ancient goddess rides on a tortoise which is described as the only living being of the primeval water.

The Gangars, a fishing tribe of lower Bengal, worships a goddess known as *Kolokumari* and the sacrifice of river tortoise forms an essential part of the ceremony; while in Gujarat, a deity called *Bahuchara* believed to be a child giver is worshipped by childless persons desirous of having their progeny. Of course, her vehicle is a cock which is a phallic symbol, an egg-maker in implication. But she is ministered by eunuch priests only who are entitled to the privileges similar to those of Gurmas, and they roam around to frequent the families where a son is born for collection of gifts as their customary claims. These are indicative of the fact that *Kolokumari* and mother goddess *Bahuchara* might be the nearest kins of Darai.

In this background, it can be reasonably presumed that deity Darai in her present form is a deity of fertility. The fact that she is worshipped before or after begetting a child is a pointer in this regard. The name of the deity might have been derived from *dura* which denotes a hard-shelled tortoise, or from the local Sylheti word *dar* meaning the deepest portion of the river or lake. *Ali* in local dialect means mother. Thus, Darai may mean "the tortoise mother" or "the mother-deity of the deep," having aquatic moorings. The logic behind the transformation of a water-deity into a deity of fertility is not a far-fetched one. In the beginning, the fishing community might have been worshipping her as a water-deity for enormous multiplication of fish so as to catch them in abundant lot. Such fertility aspect, initially confined to the aquatic world, must have found its way through primitive psyche magnifying the supernatural powers of the deity and attributing them in other correlated areas of human life, viz., germination and procreation. Thus, Darai has been enabled to widen her dominion and take over as a mother goddess and bestower of child to a zealot. The magical utilization of eggs during the heightened moment of the rites-ceremony strengthens this contention.

We would like to approach this point from a slightly different angle. As elucidated above, the Dimasas consider eggs (*daodi*) as the symbol of creation and after the birth of a child a Dimasa midwife breaks the egg with a single stroke; this breaking-act is considered to be the beginning of life of the new-born baby. Of course, ritual use of eggs is strictly forbidden in orthodox Brahamanical rites, but to the primitive people 'an egg is regarded as the symbol of new life and fertility'. According to the Dimasa folklore, life on this planet originated on the banks of the rivers. The word Dimasa itself means the sons of the great river. They have great reverence for water which is noticed when the

Dimasas purify themselves by touching *digather* which means pure water; they propitiate the spirits on the river-side only. Thus, it will be evident that these two elements,—water and egg—are compatible and complementary to each other so far as creation and fertility are concerned as per the mechanism of primitive mind. Therefore, the convergence of water-deity into a deity as offspring-giver is in the fitness of things.

In this context, the observation of E. O. James is quite pertinent to note: "The custom may have arisen from the belief that water spirits are the bestower of life and fertility, whose kindly gifts of rain from above and springs from below produce pasture for the cattle and fruit for services of men.... As authors of fertility in general, it is in accordance with the working of the primitive mind that these water spirits should come to be regarded as the bestower of offspring".

*   *   *   *

Now, the question to an ordinary mind remains as to what are the special characteristics or the virtues the Gurma possess that only he alone can act as a priest in this ritual. Even the votaries of Darai have no categorical answer, and they point towards some uncanny gifts or inborn ingenuity they acquired through their supernatural tie with the deity by virtue of their being natural eunuchs. Therefore, the Gurma came to be considered as a sort of goddess sent wizard or her authoritative agent. In fact, the devotees normally follow the tradition without the faintest idea of its evolution.

In order to trace the origin of the tradition, we may have a glimpse into the life-style of this institution and explore other regions where such practice had been widespread in the past eras.

The eunuch-dancers in the eastern, western or northern India mostly live in groups or in ghettos preferably in distant habitat-like hideouts wherefrom their unnatural or homosexual activities are not noticed by the common man and they survive on charity given by families when they are blessed with a baby. Instances of groups of eunuchs forcing people to shell out huge amounts of money at the time of marriages, festivals or other happy occasions, and even turning violent if required, are common in western Uttar Pradesh, Punjab and Haryana.

Eunuchs in India, Pakistan, Bangladesh and Nepal prefer a faminine life-style and sing and dance for a living while in other parts of the world they live a normal life. With their long hair, they wear stylish coiffure adorned with a pendant flower or strings of flowers around it or partings made with well knit braids swinging up to the hips; they use fine cosmetics and wear full blown etiquette female-dress. Keeping voluptuous smile lingering on their plump face and ever-ready mocking twinkle in their eyes, they move around perfectly with such pleasing feminine demeanor of graceful gait, pomp and modes of expression that one may be thrown into illusion for a moment gaping and gasping at such seeming blonde.

Since eunuchs lead the life of a 'sanyasi' they are not cremated but buried. Eunuchs, however, do not carry their dead to the graveyard, themselves, leaving the task to the surrounding neighbours instead. The life savings of the dead are used for celebrations and 'halwa roti' is distributed on the tenth day. However, on the 40th day eunuchs from nearby areas, and on the first death anniversary from across the country, gather for celebrations. Death seems to be the only event to rejoice in the life of eunuchs. This is a celebration of the end of a futile life and even lakhs are spent when a 'gaddidar guru' (chieftain) dies.

The Gurmas or eunuch-dancers of Cachar-Sylhet lead scattered and isolated life, on the periphery of the society. However, once they are drawn and plunged into the streams of street-life, their loud gibes and lewd behaviour become public jests. Sometimes, they look haggard, deviants and sexual pervert, and suffer from dementia praecox posing loathsome appearance. They drag the life of drudgery as their counterparts in other parts of the country and their living abodes are hideous, deplorable. They are considered social outcasts, shunned in the modern society, totally weaning out of this social institution except for a few pockets in this region associated with mother-deity as such.

In west India and the Mediterranean regions, at least three mother-goddesses viz., the Greek Artemis, the Roman Cybele and and the Syrian Astarte were used to be ministered by eunuch priests, who were not natural eunuchs, but eventually emasculated by themselves so as to seek entry into the services of those mother-goddesses. We find a vivid description of the festival of Astarte in Frazer's 'The Golden Bough' rendering the event of self-castration by onlookers to express their allegiance to faith and merge with the spirit of the cult. The spectator is enthused to join instantly the fraternity of the eunuch priests while the flutes played, the drums beat and the eunuch priests slashed themselves with knives. The religious excitement gradually spread like a wave among the crowd of onlookers and many a one did that which he little thought to do when he came as a holiday spectator to the festival. For man after man, his vein throbbing with the music, his eyes fascinated by the sight of the streaming blood, flung his garments from him, leapt forth with a shout, and seizing one of the swords which stood ready for the purpose, castrated himself on the spot. Among Red Indians, in America, it was customary to render the would-be priests impotent by depriving their virility during their childhood so as to become ministers of their female deities.

The different epochs have witnessed this tradition persisting in different regions with two common factors. First, only the eunuch priests are the ministers of female deities, and secondly they clad themselves in female attire. Therefore, Darai and her eunuch priesthood seem to have their roots in the origin of such traditional practice prevalent elsewhere. In Encyclopaedia of Religion and Ethics, Farnell has convincingly analysed to put forth a rationale for the process of eunuch priesthood: "Even the self-mutilation necessary for the attainment of the status of the eunuch priest may have arisen from the ecstatic craving to assimilate oneself to the goddess and to charge oneself with her power, the female dress being thereupon assumed to complete the transformation".

* * * *

Before concluding our study by examining the validity of the above statement , we shall delve into another similar custom prevalent in this tribal milieu. The cult of Manasa, Goddess of Snakes, probably originated in Bengal and is still largely confined to eastern India. The popular Manasa myth ascribes an aquatic birth of Manasa, and she has been described as the sister of Basuki, the lord of the nether world. She is, by association, a goddess of fertility, and may be prevailed upon to cure snake bites.

Darai being a deity associated with water and fisherman who holds two snakes in her two hands, is destined to be absorbed in the more dominating cult of this snake-goddess Manasa. Actually often people use the term Darai Bishahari to denote Manasa. The sculpted figure of Manasa in bronze with inlay (Pala·period, c.750 AD) preserved in the British Museum, London, depicts not only both her hands holding snakes, but a canopy of five cobra-heads rearing above her head. The sexual grace and power with which such figures of Darai and Manasa are charged is in part a representation of fertility; but it is also a complementary disguise designed to assure these powerful forces that they are thought to be beautiful and are suitably admired. Flattery, whether verbal or visual, is a part of the propitiation process.

Beneath the tangled roots of trees lie the subterranean waters, the haunt of serpents. Here are the hidden treasures of the earth and it is from this darkness that the tree and all terrestrial life arises. The multiform, colourful world of man grows out of the uniform dark, the formless waters. Inhabiting both these worlds, gliding from one to the other, symbol of their interconnection is the snake, swift and silent, limbless and deadly. This sign of transition is vital to man, who must be assured that his world is a cohesive unity, he cannot exist in chaos. So, the snake connects the world of man with the nether world.

So was it in ancient times, and the survival of this element in the pattern is evident everywhere in later religious art, cosmology and philosophy too. In images of the Hindu God Vishnu the moment before the creation of the universe, he is depicted lying in a yogic sleep upon the serpent Ananta, 'Endless', with its multiple cobra-heads forming a canopy above him. This serpent represents the oceanic, undifferentiated condition of the raw material of creation (*pralaya*) before it is polarized and developed through a series of transformations stimulated by the female energy of the god. Nagas-cult figures of the serpent-rulers of the underworld–whether depicted alone or dominated by the high gods or goddesses in such composite images—assumed a standard form right from the 2nd century BC.

As a sculpted image, the *naga* presence in a temple is always believed to be auspicious, being a part of the ancient pattern of natural phenomenon which imitates the wild and so sanctifies all holy places. It also invokes human and agricultural fertility, and at the same time, paradoxical as this may seem, protects the worshipper from snakes. While the *naga* is a symbol, snakes are real and deadly. By worshipping and placating the *nagas* in the temple, a measure of protection from real snakes in the forests and fields is obtained.

The Hindu God Shiva is regarded as a healer of venomous infection, being called—among his many other epithets—Vishapaharana, 'Remover of Poison'. With this background of symbolic values of snakes, Manasa, the goddess of snakes, has to be viewed and interpreted at manifold levels in a wider context. She is not only regarded as Bishahari, 'Remover of Poison' as enunciated above, but a protector to her devotees against the snakes, and as fertilizing deity too. Here, also the Gurma had the monopoly of *Manasa Mangal* recital, performed at the occasion of

Manasa worship, the reason being that Darai has been actually worshipped in the image of Manasa. The role of the Gurmas in the recital of *Manasa Mangal* is simply a corollary to this process of absorption. Though not much expurgation from obscenity, the Gurma displays here better taste and adroitness.

During the month of *Shravan,* the month sacred to Manasa, the recital of *Manasa Mangal* is an overwhelming household affair and the professional eunuchs are found scarce to meet the growing demand. Therefore, their vocation is being taken over by another sect called *ojha.* Originally *ojhas* were village medicine men believed to be capable of curing snake bites. Naturally as devout worshippers of the snake deity, they claim to have been specially privileged as to the performance of such recital.

During the recitals, these male *ojhas* play perfect role of Gurmas presenting themselves as their exact replicas holding *chamars* in their hands and wearing female attire without which they apprehend to invite unleashing of wrath from the goddess. In order to attain ritual efficacy while substituting for the eunuchs, they transvestise themselves in female dress and in this regard they have their counterparts in other regions also. The *Pala* dancers of Orissa wear female dress. The *Mala Pujaris,* the recognised priests of local mother-deity in South India, also dress themselves in female costumes while performing the worship. In the remote lands of Tahitis and British Guinea, some tribal priests continue wearing female dress throughout their life. The ancient Crete had the biggest ratio of such priests. And, in the Aegean Civilization, 1925, G.Glotz has expounded the following views on the origin of the practice of priests wearing female attire:

"The priestesses long presided over religious practices, woman was the natural intermediary with the divinity.... the participation of men in the cult was, like the association of a god with a goddess, a late development. Their part in the religious ceremonies was always a subordinate one, even when the king became the high priest of the bull .... As if to extenuate their encroachment and not to baffle the spirits to whose power this act has exposed them, they assumed for divine services the priestly costume of woman".

The two analytical approaches propounded by Farnell and Glotz and their observations on the origin of eunuch priesthood and transvestism share common ground, out of which the glimpse of a pattern could be discerned. The process shows forth process of its evolution indicating certain stages which complete the transformation of the female priestesses into transvestite males.

Whoever may be the ministers, the fact remains that their deities are all female deities of fertility. According to Robert Briffault, the world of primitive men treated the fecundity of women equal to that of the fecundity of nature. To their mind, both are synonymous as far as their fertility is concerned. Innumerable clay images of the mother goddesses are made throughout India today as they were 4000 years ago. Among them, the earth-mother is most characteristically depicted as a roughly shaped piece of the earth itself. Here, the body ornaments and the special insistence upon tall head-dresses of flowers and plants are, of course, symbols of the vegetal fertility of the earth. Style and the degree of detail an artist was prepared to put into such images varied according to period and place, but the essential concept of a lump of the earth fashioned into a female form as personification of the fundamental first element (earth) has been unaltered for thousands of years. It was in the Indus Valley Civilization, with its widespread provincial culture, that probably the first such cult in India—no doubt the amalgamation of many—can be said to have been established. The small images were produced in their thousands, the clay quickly twisted and pinched to delineate limbs and features, the eyes, lips and indispensable ornaments merely rolled and applied. In this and most successive cultures, no matter what degree of sophistication was being attained in the artistic working of other media, the crudity of manufacture remained almost a constant. There can be little doubt that it was, and is, deliberate.

The idea working behind it was that the fertility of women was not only equated with the nature, but due to this attribute she was even exalted to the position of having divine nature in such cases. The same logic secured for the women a special position of dexterity where magical rites for fertilization were to be performed. The ancient mother-goddessess of West Asia, the Mediterranean regions and in all indigenous Indian cults were essentially deities of fertility. This concept has been powerfully translated into the image of the *nagna-kabandha* (Lotus-headed female figure of early Chalukya period, c.8th century, Andhra Pradesh), simple meaning 'naked (headless) torso', where the female generative organs and breasts are prominently displayed, the head completely replaced by a lotus.

The development of the Hindu cult of the Goddess is referred to as *shakti* worship. A composite Goddess concept evolved, incorporating various components, such as motherhood, elements of goddesses invoked in the earlier Vedas, and several indigenous strands unknown in Vedic religion. Generally, the Goddess as creative energy is identified with procreation, the power of lust and, ultimately, with spiritual liberation. In the later development of both Hindu and Buddhist Tantrism, Shakti-Devi is considered the formless, absolute principle immanent throughout the universe and is depicted as the antagonist of all evil in the eternal cosmic struggle. Whatever be the numerous forms the Goddess assumes here symbolizing the different ways in which she is conceived, the concept of mother goddess is common and dominant one amongst them everywhere. It is quite natural that these mother goddesses symbolising fertility were ministered initially by female priestesses for extracting maximum fertilising effect, simply by virtue of her said special position enshrined by the primitive men. Subsequent reign of a purely male dominated society banished the priestesses from the worshipping places. In this context, Merline Stone has aptly remarked, "It seems quite possible that as men began to gain power even within the religion of the Goddess, they replaced priestesses".

Whatever supremacy the man attained in the society in this phase, he could not dispense with the germinating fertility of the woman; as a result, her traditional role in ritual efficacy continued to remain unequal. A new sect of male ministers of the goddesses so emerged is a compromise on this count. But the imitation of the female clergy which used to hold sway over this ritual realm (sphere), must have made them to shed their maleness by resorting to castration and wearing of female dress. When the changing situation demanded, this cruel practice of emasculation was discarded, giving room for natural eunuchs to replace their castrated counterparts.

Transvestism adopted by male priests is a natural consequence to this process. If the changing situations compel the natural eunuchs to abandon the priestly profession and simultaneously the people's dogmas continue to embrace the feminine virtues in ritual proficiency, the transvestism is the most acceptable mode to compromise and to overcome the dead-end. The recital of *Manasa Mangal* by male *ojhas* in female attire in the Sylhet-Cachar regions is a glaring illustration of this transitory phase.

We have noticed the sequence of this transition, i.e. from female priestesses to castrated eunuchs, then to natural eunuchs, and finally to male transvestised in female dress, which might not be a universal phenomenon. There might be some more sequential stages somewhere, while in other cases one or two intermediate stages might be omitted or skipped. However, the theoretical formulation operative behind the origin and development of such deity-worship is uniform everywhere.

Different transitory phases are nothing but the indications of changes brought about by evolutionary process accelerated in social structure and its cultural milieu; indications of changes occurred in man, his content of consciousness and lastly his perception as a whole, that has brought him to the present state.

After ten thousand years the tribal consciousness has re-emerged in different societies, in different continents, but it's altogether a separate issue.

References

1. Freud, Sigmund, Totem and Tabu, London,1950
2. Durkheim, Emile, The Elementary forms of the religious life, 1915.
3. Middleton, John (ed.), Gods and Rituals, 1967.
4. Turner, W. Victor, The Forest of Symbols, 1967.
5. Hooke, S.H. (ed.), Myth, Ritual and Kingship, 1958.
6. Fontenrose, Joseph E., The Ritual Theory of Myth, 1966.
7. Eliade, Mircea, Birth and Rebirth, 1958.
8. Crooke, W., The Popular Religion and Folklore of Northern India, Vol. II (Reprint), Delhi, 1968.
9. Briffault, Robert, The Mothers, Vol.II, London, 1927.
10. Mackenzi, D.A., Myths from China and Japan, London, 1930.
11. Hastings, J. (ed.), Encyclopaedia of Religious Ethics, Vol-I, New York, 1973.
12. Kakati, Banikanta, Visnuite Myths and Legends, Gauhati, 1952.
13. Frazer, J.G., The Golden Bough (abridged), London, 1963.
14. Pike, E.R., The Strange Ways of Man, New York, 1967.
15. Leach, Maria, The Standard Dictionary of Folklore, Mythology and Legend, Vol. I, New York, 1949.
16. British Advisory Committee and Indian Advisory Committee: In the Image of Man, New Delhi, Vikas Publishing House Pvt. Ltd, 1982.
17. Whitehead, H., The Village God of South India, Calcutta, 1921.
18. Stone, Merlin, The Paradise Papers, London, 1977.

Chapter 7

Folk Songs

Any kind of singing is universal in human society; it is a manifestation of finer aspects of human life. Often, poems and songs give us a clearer insight into a people's soul than the most lengthy discussions. And, in the poetry of those unlettered and unsophisticated lie certain important clues to their philosophy of life. Even though the folksongs are used simply for the pleasure of singing or listening, they also act as the medium for the expression of ideas or emotions held in common by a group. A community, whether agricultural or otherwise, expresses itself passionately and imaginatively through its folksongs. These songs are live human documents reflecting actual historical processes and phenomena of different ages. Though the relationship between the members of a community or a group, in some cases, must have been based purely on their basic necessities, the super-structures of religion, philosophy and literature also penetrated deep into the reality of their social situation as is seen in much of the world everywhere. Therefore, the cultural traits of their rich folk heritage can be discerned mostly in their folksongs and rhymes.

As a matter of fact, in many places these songs are of great importance and sung at the functionally important junctures of various rituals ranging from harvest festivals to marriages, births and deaths; while in certain regions, the songs are used to infatuate and enrapture the hearts of lovers or to serve as a part of religious ceremonies and secular rites, or to depict past exploits of the heroes. Through them, the group also lighten the burden of communal labour. In some preliterate groups, the songs are used as recital of incantations to invoke blessings from the supernatural powers, or for magical effects to cure illness, or to thwart enemies.

Folk songs imply the use of music, and the musical tradition varies greatly from one area to another. Few aspects of human culture can claim to be so old and so universal as music. Being present in all the human societies from very ancient times, music has unfolded in diverse forms. But it has a special role to play in the primitive society since non-ritualistic or magico-religious music became quite developed at one stage of their civilization in certain continents. When the language was not much developed in the earlier stages of our society, man relied upon vocal tunes to communicate with supernatural powers to supplicate for his prosperity and protection from evils. With gradual emergence of the trend of singing 'worded songs', this powerful medium became more effective, to exploit its non-ritualistic aspect to express different human feelings, apart from its tantric use to obtain some tangible results. In some places words of songs are of little importance and seem to be used primarily as support for the music. Frequently there are senseless monosyllables and much repetition to accompany the voice or the musical instrument. In most parts of the world, drums and rattles, beating time by hands or feet or the stroking of a harp give a strong rhythmic effect to folk-singing. In others, flute-like wind instruments or single-stringed bamboo fiddle or bowed fiddles of one kind or another are used to affect the nature of the folk-song texts.

It needs special mention here that the collateral use of music and folk-songs is greatly valued among certain preliterate groups for curative propitiation and exorcistic seance-purposes. In most of such songs, one spirit or the other is invoked. The utterances are generally made with conviction, urgency and sincerity. Actual ownership of such songs is invariably maintained and their use carefully guarded. They may come to the owner in a dream or as the result of fasting or other austerities.

Even when folk songs and music are not used for those practical purposes but only for the pleasure of singing or listening, the greater part of the world uses them for expressions of commonly shared ideas or feelings which are often trivial but sometimes they may be profoundly moving. It so happens that the songs, though inherited from the past, would be having a different orientation in their spirit in the sense that the ideas, composition and notation for them were conceived in consonance with the prevailing cultural-contact situation in most of the places. With the advent of speedy means of communication, the interaction between different peoples of remotest areas became more vibrant especially at the levels of socio-economic and socio-political life. The continuity of these contacts became more dynamic so much so that the felt need of the social life of these people was the orientation in the mode of expression of various cultural elements that they had. The result is palpable in the structures, tunes and themes of their folksongs including those sometimes spontaneously composed. Similarly, preliterate societies used music as an unambiguous signal for expressing human thoughts more than as a finer symbol, apart from using it to please his companions, and for his personal pleasure and relief as an entertainer. It is, therefore, expected that culture will be reflected more in the music of a man who is in more primitive condition. Here, the music is born out of free vein of human sensibilities unlike its modern trend based on conscious systematisation and codification with a view to reaching an impersonal transcendental world of aesthetics.

Thus the accompaniment of folksongs or such music can be rightly categorized as folk level melody being a folk level thinking which is quite distinct from classical or 'absolute music' that can be classified as 'art level melody' being at an art level thinking. Having wider scope, the former achieves deeper penetration in the world of thoughts, whereas the latter being more 'codified' and abstract is accessible to a limited circle of its specialization.

Only in societies used to the songs of composers or poets does purely personal expression enter into the folk song. This is not frequent, and songs of this type are hardly to be distinguished from some of the simple lyrics of poets such as Robert Burns. However, quite different from this type are the lyric folk songs in one form or another found almost everywhere, but this is not true of narrative singing. In a varying degree, akin to such combination of song and story, are the dance-songs among preliterate cultures chanted by the full complement of a race or a social institution from the youngest boy to the oldest warrior who can still swing a decorative lethal weapon and bend his knees in the rhythm of the festive round dance. Pride in one's own race or social institution is expressed in numerous songs praising the might and prowess of its mythical or historical figures; here tales are not described but only alluded to, so as to arouse emotional associations rather than amusing an audience indicating the mythical background and are consequently understandable only to the initiated.

In traditional literature of Garo in North East India, the art of the poet, called *Tuara Nangapa,* is developed on similar lines. Here, incantations and narratives are all sung to a tune and all of them, except the folk tales, are in verse form. Tunes differ according to localities and dialects, but all use verse forms comprising narratives, songs and incantations, slightly different from each other and possessing the characteristics of fine poetry-figurative language, rhyme and measured lines. The stylistics of this *Katta Agana* evolved and perfected and handed down by the forefathers through generations is a typical specimen narrating the origin of Dikki, their cultural hero, and expressing their extraordinary ancestry.

In major Western and Asian civilizations the narrative song has been important for a long time and has been cultivated by the most skillful singers. Such songs of warfare, of adventure, or of domestic life have formed local cycles, such as the *byliny* of Russia or the heroic songs of Yugoslavia and Finland, ballad tradition of western Europe and elsewhere. In India, Manipuri *Moirangsayon* has seven cycles concerning seven incarnations (*Sayon*) of two lovers of Moi-lang. The story of Khamba and Thoibi is in the seventh part of that cycle. Khamba and Thoibi, regarded as deities, personify ideal Meithei hero and woman.

Each of such cycles has its own characteristics, with its distinctive metrical forms, and its formulas both of events and expressions. Early literary narratives of Sumer, the Near East and the Homeric poems suggest a long previous development of narrative singing, essentially oral and of musical nature.

HUMANISTIC APPROACH

In this approach, the humanistic folklorist considers the materials of folklore as "oral literature" and the folk as artistic performers of tale or song. He emphasizes the creative role of the narrator or minstrel, gathers information on his biography and personality, very closely observes his interaction with the audience, and analyzes his total repertoire much as a literary critic assesses the achievement of the novelist, poet, or dramatist. We find the exponents of this approach from among the older generation particularly from departments of modern language and literature or music or classic. Albert Lord, Professor of Slavic literature at Harvard University, has done pioneering works on folklore after collecting and studying oral epics, still sung by bards in Yugoslavia. His "oral-formulaic" theory expounded that each epic singer constructed his narrative song by improvising and elaborating around a stock of fixed images, epithets, and conventional expressions, which he alone kept firmly in mind. He applied this theory to the Homeric epics which are now in their written forms, but which, he conjectured, had been orally composed in the same manner as the contemporary Slavic epic songs. The other humanistic folklorists applied Lord's theory to various traditional texts—from Norwegian ballads to the Anglo-Saxon epic Beowulf to medieval romances, after appearance of Lord's work, 'The Singer of Tales' (1960). The interest in the human carrier of tradition, in his world-view and belief system, his cultural inheritance and acculturative experiences, distinguishes this species of folklorists.

Folklore to anthropological folklorist is an aesthetic product of this society, mirroring its values and offering a projective screen that illuminates its fantasies. Here, he frequently reports a one-to-one correlation between the value system and the tale repertoire of a given culture, which has its parallel in some of the Indian so-called post-modernist trends in literature widely known as *nativism* or *deshivad* flourishing on complete content-orientiation. While controverting the views of folkloristic anthropologist, the humanistic approach points out that the same tales are found in many parts of the globe and so can scarcely be said to reflect the ethos of a particular people, even when they have been strongly localized.

The former looks for cultural norms and values and predictable laws of behaviour that form a consistent pattern in the nonliterate society he has closely observed. However, this approach posed difficulty in encompassing the materials of folklore within a culture almost wholly oral and traditional. William Bescom, a student of Herskovits, coined the term 'verbal art' to denote the oral aesthetic traditions of tales, proverbs, songs and riddles in the culture, leaving out the supernatural-belief system and the plastic arts, which humanistic folklorist includes in his concept.

In order to interpret the folk songs particularly from North East India, the help of both these perspectives has been sought to such an extent that the boundaries between the two will be found totally blurred. At times, even though one perspective is exclusively applied, full treatment as required under the same has not been given while understanding the song. Only the most interesting cultural traits reflected in the song with its realm of legend, its lyricism, finest human sentiments and the subtlety of expression have been brought under scrutiny leaving aside other areas to be explored by folklore-minded anthropologists and other scholars for their research as it is beyond the scope of the study. Of course, to those unfamiliar with the tribal psyche, their ways of life, their ancient traditions and cultural ethos, the full appreciation of certain songs and their poetical language seems to be denied due to obvious reasons. Therefore, general characteristics of the people, significant background and contexts of the songs and ethnolingual peculiarities are shown in a nutshell, wherever necessary, so as to make their frequent meanings more illuminating and appealing to the initiated and perceptive mind. As a whole, endeavour is made to keep humanistic approach dominant throughout.

Repetition and vocal interpolations are the traits typical to folk songs in North East India. Sometimes, the songs, though sung in good spirit, are monotonous and dull, rather like dirges, and sometimes, enchanting and vigorous, accompanied by dance in romp and playing musical instruments with great hilarity, at the same time keeping rhythmic beat with a little bark on a high shrill note.

All the festivals and social functions are celebrated by feasting, dancing, and singing by different communities of this region. So also, special occasions such as marriage and birth of a child consist of similar festivities in many cases, as in the case of Assamese. Nagas dressed up in ceremonial clothes and ornaments used to celebrate victory in war (head-hunting) and Feasts of Merit by brisk feasting, dancing and singing. Spring festival (birth of spring) is greatly valued among Konyak Nagas. On the day of the celebration, crowd of men, whirling their spears and *dao* as though setting out on the war path, rush through the village with wild cries. With their tossing feathers, and the gaily dyed goat's hair waving from weapons and head-dress they look like fantastic birds, and, like birds in the mating season, they rejoice in the glory of their brilliant spring dress, that reduces the weaker sex to comparative insignificance. Village-open place is thronged with singing crowds of men. *Dao* flash high in the air, voices are raised, and the song swells forth, breaking at times into temperamental outbursts, and at the climax into harsh, uncanny yells.

Various languages abound in folksongs of this part of the country. The songs in many cases are sung couched in archaic language considerably different from ordinary spoken language and sometimes the meaning has been entirely forgotten. Dr. J.H. Hutton has rightly observed: "Where it is remembered the meaning of the song as a whole is often obscure, as the composer of a song uses disconnected words which mean much to him but convey little to those who cannot follow his thoughts and do not know what he is alluding to. Even newly composed songs often need their composer to explain exactly what it is all about, and trying to translate them with the aid of someone who does not happen to know is rather like trying to disentangle a difficult chorus of Aeschylus".

Man and Nature

Arunachal Pradesh is unique so far as its folk heritage is concerned. Though the larger canvas is Tibeto-Burman, the indigenous population is divided under different group names, with distinct ethno-linguistic heritage which, along with their special ecological set-up modifying their thinking pattern, echoes in their verses. These tribes neither can supply the elaborate meanings of their songs nor can they translate a word or a phrase. Mere singing of the songs correctly seems to be more important to them than the lexiconic meanings of the words. While extricating their thought patterns, hills and rivers are the two watchwords that we come across reverberating in the life of the people of this hilly-terrain. Other natural objects such as trees, flowers and stars are also eternally repeated in their folk songs whose examples are given below:

Both of us are friends and have grown simultaneously like old trees during the same period of time. We are searching pleasure and laughing together. We are happy but not equal like those stars in the sky (as they seem from far). I think people think us same when they listen to us laughing and doing fun together. But when the stars could become equal, we could not.

(Nishi—Arunachal Pradesh)

O, as so many stars,
As the sun rises,
The sun in the sky,
O, Yana and Shayong's sons,
So high are they in the sky.
O, like the high trees
Like the virgin forest,
O, Yana and Shayong's sons,
Great are they on the earth.

(Konyak—Nagaland)

On the eve of new year, the flowers on the high hills on the other side are glistening as if the sun is rising there. Let us hope that all the goods and evils of the past year will have a new meaning in this new year and let our life be as bright as the blooming flowers on the hills.

(Monpa— Arunachal Pradesh)

People will rejoice
Be rejoice, people;
Like flowers blossom at hill top.
How lovely is the blossom at hill top.

At the hill top,
Be seen by all the world.
Insurmountable delight;
Be delightful.

(Khiamnungans—Nagaland)

Good new friend,
Friendship that made in jungle
Good new friend,
Friendship that made on the way.
Destine to die,
So make friend all along the way.
Like the flowers blossom,
Let the friendship blossom.

(Yimchunger—Nagaland)

Flower, fully bloomed flower,
alone you are blooming, alone wilting,
our age also has reached youth,
alone it is wilting.

(Kachari—Assam)

There is no natural world set apart from man. In the distant past, the mighty 'Lord of the Forest', Vanaspati, tallest of trees was praised in ritual chants; and those few trees, spared at the outskirts of the human settlement were taken as sacred, standing between bright heaven and this world, between the circle of civilization and the savage tribes of Rudra deep in the dark forest beyond, as the direct link between the eternal unitary sun and this world-haunted transiently, yet continuously, by the generations and tribes of man.

He who separates himself from all this life is a shadow; he neither knows nor is known; he is the outsider, feared and spurned. Exile in the community in the midst of life is a living death. Thus, in India all life is embraced. It is the same life current which flows from the sun, and from the rivers, which courses through all that lives : rock, earth, trees, water, fire, cloud, air, light and dark.

The force of life is naturally symbolized by the growing configuration of trees in Nishi and Konyak songs above, the former signifying the growth and perpetual change, while the latter is devoted to the praise of the descendants who are likened to stars and sun, and to the high trees of the virgin forest. The Nishi poet has gone one step further to depict the nature, cosmic pattern in its equality governed by the law of uniformity man is pitted against with his nature of inequality, duality and therefore, divisions, though different apparently look so similar. The theme reveals the state of discord resulting from otherness inherent between two persons who are friendly and outwardly happy enjoying together which is nothing but the semblance of reality contrasted with the cosmic phenomenon. Therefore, in one Monpa song, the poet has accentuated the bond of friendship to be as immutable as that of never changing shape of sun. However, in contradiction to all, one of the Miji songs has discerned universal differences not only in the mental make-up of two persons, but even in the nature itself, viz., hills, flowing of water, flowers etc. which is, as implied, basic to the natural law preponderant everywhere.

The powerful imagery of flowers recurring in the Monpa song—flowers on the high hills, so glowing and lustrous as if the rising sun, dispelling the darkness and endowing new dimension to the good and the evils of the past–is laden with rich ambiguity of multi-layer meanings; the metaphorical image signifies hope, immense joy, and blooming and flourishing the life with exuberance, its all-pervasive luscious fragrance and all-round glory ahead, in the new year. The poem expresses the optimistic world-view of a tribal mind with the texture of human aesthetic.

In Khiamnungans song, not the life but the people themselves are vividly delineated as a mass of flowers, sprightly luminous on hill-top; then, not the beautiful people, but only the wealth of ecstacy of the living spirit of nature, as though with a soul, in its splendour and such majesty that the whole world enthralled would behold at it. As is the hill-top, so is the delight unsurmountable. Here, the perception involves transformation of the spirit of man into unsurpassable animated nature and its dynamism itself.

Contrary to the above, in the Yimchunger and Kachari songs, the projection of the blossoming flower image has grim overtones in the background. While in the former, the poet advocates to make friendship in the journey of life, either in the jungle or by the wayside, since life is at all times vulnerable to hazards and is mortal, and therefore let it be allowed to bloom like flowers, the latter portrays the transitoriness of life which culminating in prime youth and then withering away the same way as a flower after having fully bloomed begins to shrivell away to nothing, which carries underlying note of despair.

Against the cosmic panorama, man has often tried to fathom himself in relation to mystery of nature, its invincibility and vagaries, its occasional outrage and eternal grandeur; he has tried to evince himself to be combative, sometimes in his unending quest, imagined to be transferred into embodiment of nature's immortal elements or has been in conflict with it and subdued, overcome by utter hopelessness which are all evident in his songs of joys and sorrows, hopes and predicaments. Thus, he has been defining himself and his fraternity in the world of human bondage. The preliterate man had remained in constant communion with nature.

Love

Love is an inexhaustible theme in Konyak folk-songs. Of course, many songs are fully understandable only to a limited circle and even the singers sometimes can not explain the exact meaning of the individual words, for the archaic language used in songs is very different from the language in everyday use. Over and above, Konyak , as other languages of the Tibeto-Burman group, has a complicated tonal system. Nagas of neighbouring tribes comment on the great difference between the Konyak dialects and their own languages. They resort to Nagamese, the *lingua franca,* during their conversation with Konyaks. Therefore, recording and translation of their innumerable songs meet with peculiar difficulties "just as the spoken language varies from village to village so greatly that within a radius of ten miles one may find three distinct dialects, so too differ the poetical idioms not only of villages, but even of individual *morung* ," observes Christopher Von Furer-Haimendorf. Yet these are no longer dead idioms preserved only in traditional formulas, for today the young men and women still compose new songs spontaneously in the same stereotyped phrases, though they are unable to give a word-for-word translation.

Songs are the principal and recognised medium through which the individual as well as the group express their most intense emotions. However, a curious gap in the range of Konyak songs is the absence of working chants. Nagas of most other tribes sing at work on the fields or when carrying loads, and in the Angami area at planting time the work songs of boys and girls resound from all the rice-terraces and fill the valleys from morning to evening. The Konyaks, on the other hand, do not sing at work: when they drag in a huge house-pole it is to rhythmic yells and shouts, and young people weeding the hill-crops will break into cascades of laughter and shrieks but never into song.

It is only at night when the boys visit the girls in their dormitories, that they spend hours singing. And when at dusk the young people return from work from the fields they assemble on the raised platforms specially built for this purpose at all entrances to the village : boys and girls, leaning affectionately against each other, sing alternate songs, each vying with the other in appropriate responses, and their verses, sometimes sentimental, sometimes taunting, always exploiting perennial theme of love. Just go through some examples:

Boys : We have come to your house to sing,
Tell us frankly whether you want us as your lovers;
Do not tease us, by saying one thing,
And doing another.

Girls : Alas, we can only love you for a few months,
For we are betrothed to our cousins,
And it would be wicked to break the engagement.

Boys : We do not want to be your lovers
For a short time only;
We want to have you for all time
As our wives.

Girls : We cannot be your wives,
Our parents would be cross with us
If we did so.

Boys : We have offered to become your husbands,
But you want only temporary lovers;
So we shall go to other girl's houses.
Girls : Well, go ahead and make love to them
If you can get other girls,
We too can get other lovers.

Boys : At first you talked very sweetly,
But now you have turned us down
And we feel very bitter.
We will not waste our time with you,
But go in search of other girls.

Girls : We did not know that you wanted to marry us,
We thought you only wanted to love us.
You never told us what was in your mind.
We were quite willing to make love to you
For a few months, but we cannot be your wives.
For we are already betrothed to our cousins
And they would feel bad if we broke the engagement.

Our mother's brother would beat us,
And we are afraid of him.

Boys : Be it so. We love you all too much
And if you do not want to marry us,
Let us be your lovers for some time.

(Konyak—Nagaland)

This song shows clearly that love affairs not leading to marriage were normal experiences in a girl's life, even though she might have been betrothed to a cross-cousin. The tenor of the chant, which seemed to combine traditional features with skilful improvisation, reflected very cearly the young people's attitude to premarital romance as well as the obligations resulting from kinship ties and a pattern of preferential marital unions between cross-cousins. The song highlights a girl's willingness to enjoy such premarital adventures, though brief, with a number of lovers without committing herself to a more permanent union, and suggests that young men were more keener on marriage than the girls. On the whole, free and easy relations between the unmarried of both sexes echo from the alternating chants.

At night hours, once the boys are in the dormitory and sit on the bamboo benches by the side of a pleasant fire, their arms round the waists of their girl friends, the songs become more straight forward and direct :

Girls of the other *morung,*
O, our friends,
In your mother's hand
Money and jewels ;
In your husband's hand
Little or nothing.
Once you have borne
Two or three children
Gone is the beauty of your body.

Love your friends,
Love the friends of your youth.

And a girl answers :

When you are with me,
Your tears flow;
When you are with your wife,
You smile and laugh.
Why, leaving your wife,
Have you come to me ?
Her you love more
Than the friends of your youth.

(Konyak—Nagaland)

In the first stanzas of the song, the boys exhort their girl friends to adore the loves of their youth showing them the abject life in the husband's house in contrast to the gaiety and galore lavished by mother's care. The "money and jewels in the mother's hand" signify affluence and luxuries rolling around under the parental upbringing. The Konyak girls are gifted with exceedingly beautiful, gracious bodies and they are proud of the charms of their slim figures. To make them conscious of their beauty which would be waning away after giving birth to two or three children is not only to show married life detestable, but also to cajole for enamouring love for the friends of their youth. But the inherent irony of the fate that their love might impregnate them causing painful separation has been lost sight of or deliberately ignored.

In the second of the songs, a girl mocks at her love that he is more amorous to his wife than to her. The first four lines carry double meanings. "Your tears flow" may be interpreted as begging of her love or narrating the woes and discord of his married life, while "you smile and laugh" is a sarcastic remark on his over-joy that he finds in his wife's embrace or the frolic and fun that he cuts of her during coupling with his wife. Here, the love-seekers who draw so sullen a picture of married life are themselves married, and yet free-birds and philanderers.

Moshup life is rich in love and it would have been surprising if such a musical people as the Adis would have had no expression for it in songs. Actually, there is a large number of such songs, but they are difficult to get at because they are sung in seclusion and privacy. There is many a love-lorn swain who sings amorous melodies to his sweetheart behind granary or in a secluded corner of the *rasheng*. These he will rarely sing in public. Such an outpour of the heart is meant solely for the ear of the beloved. There are also compositions in alternating dialogue from where both pour out the yearnings of their heart to each other.

Among the boys there,
who is he who matches me
in age and status ?
Oh ! could he be mine !
Oh ! what a joy it would be
if we could sit together at night
and I could have him close.
I like him for his age and beauty.
How I wish he would like me -
Oh ! how it could be done !
It would be nice if his heart
inclines the way as mine.

Among the girls there,
Who is she who
matches me -
in age and status ?
How could I win her !
Oh ! what a joy it would
be
if our houses were close
and we could always be
near each other.
She is quite my match.
Oh ! my friends, just tell
me.
how I could win her.
It would be nice if her
heart and mind grow
one and the same.

(Adis—Arunachal Pradesh)

Many Naga songs are straightforward descriptions of the romantic love. Here is one Sema Naga song illustrating such a situation. Not only Konyak poetry but such other Naga songs are also couched in archaic poetical language, and though on traditional lines, they are mostly spontaneous compositions. However, the addition of meaningless words of *Ho holo iye hele, ole iyi le he-e* etc. mingled in the texture of Lotha songs make the chanting more melodious and pleasing but impossible to understand the meaning of those songs without the full details of the circumstances to which they relate. But they are completely discarded in all such lyrics so as to achieve resonance and to make them enchanting with very great appeal.

In Sema song, the boy sings and the girl in response asks him to pluck a piece of orchid in the rift. Here, the flower denoting delicacy, fragrance and beauty is a vehicle of lover's desire to be plucked. Often invitation to 'test her' from one's utmost where all other tastes are comparatively of no use and, therefore, meaningless since our sensory capacity is incomplete to reach this region, aims at transporting the lover from the sensory to the non sensory realm, thus, straining beyond the known boundaries of physical eroticism to the depth of 'heart and soul.' To grasp her as a whole, requires to extend the boundaries of the individual senses until they meet and coalesce. Here, the 'test' operates at synaesthetic level too.

Dear, walk in front of me.
Dear, walk in front of me.
Good water flows from ridges,
Good water flows from stony land.
If you really love,
Test me by your utmost.
All your tests will be of no use,
Since I love you with my whole heart and soul.

There is a flower on the tree top,
There is a flower on the tree top,
There is an orchid in the rift.
Dear, pluck it for me please.

* Name of a particular woman

Dear, wear it and be beauty
There is no cord how to wear on my ear,
Dear give me the one with cord please,
Alas ! there is none with cord.

(Sema—Nagaland)

A few couplets from Angami poem which the lovers sing while strolling at the edge of jungle or collecting wild vegetables are rendered here in free translation.

To part with you
Is heart breaking,
How can I go,
Where I can not see you.

As full grown paddy stalk in field,
Dancing in the breeze of summer,
So as you are, my darling,

To the sweet heart under heaven,
Who can be double minded.
Ruditsou,* scatter seeds from your beautiful hand,
To grow as beautiful as you are.
To all places I go for courting,
I met not one fairer than you,
You have captured my heart.

Loudly, I would have called you darling,
But if some of your lovers hear me,
They will question you again,
That's why I am cautious.

If I come to court you one night,
If your neighbours ask you the next morning,
Who visited you last night ?
Be reserved, betray not, confuse them.

(Angami—Nagaland)

In her dancing playfulness, the girl is described here as an essential part of nature, her unwitting wantonness of beauty the very power of *prakriti*—the inherent dynamism of the wild—which captivates the lover's heart. Rather than becoming possessive, the lover is cautious and warns her against exposing him so as to guard her free sports with her other loves.

The Bhuiyas in the north of the Brahmaputra, the boundary between Kamrup and the ancient Matsyadesh, and the surroundings of the Parisnath hill in Manbhum and Hazaribagh districts have their peculiar dance-features, but as compared with the vivacious and graceful movements of the Kols, they are very tame performances.

The men have each a rude kind of tambourine. They march round in a circle, beating these and singing a very simple melody in a minor key on four notes. The women dance opposite to them with their heads covered and bodies much inclined, touching each other like soldiers in line, but not holding hands or wreathing arms. The more exciting and exhilarating occasions are when the young men of one village proceed to visit the maidens of another village, or when the maidens return the call. The young men, going straight to the *darbar*–a dancing ground of the village they visit, proclaim their arrival loudly by beating their drums or tambourines. The girls of that village immediately join them. Their male relations and neighbours must keep entirely out of view, leaving the field clear for the guests.

The offerings of the visitors are now gallantly presented and graciously accepted, and the girls at once set to work to prepare dinner for their beaux, and after the meal they dance and sing and flirt all night together, and the morning dawns on more than one pair of pledged lovers. Then the girls, if the young men have conducted themselves to their satisfaction, make ready the morning meal for themselves and their guests; after which the latter rise to depart, and still dancing and playing on the drums, move out of the village followed by the girls, who escort them to the boundary. This is generally a rockbroken stream with wooded banks; here they halt, the girls on one side, the lads on the other, and to the accompaniment of the babbling brook sing to each other in true bucolic style. The song on these occasions is to a certain extent improvised, and is a pleasant mixture of raillery and love-making. A specimen is given below :

Boys
A kanchan flower bring to us,
We'll listen whilst you sing to us.

Girls
We'll gather greens for dinner, dear !
But cannot think of singing here.

Boys
As Radha's pretty little bird,
You sweetly sing and must be heard.

Girls
You silken meshes o'er us fling,
But truly, love ! we cannot sing.

Boys
A handful that of chaff and straw,
Us boys you surely beat at jaw !

Girls (pouting)
Ah ! birds that chirp and fly away !
With us you care not than to stay ?

Boys (amorous)
Yes, yes, we've caught some pretty fish,
To part, dear girls, is not our wish.

Girls (pleased)
The clouds disperse, the day look fair,

Come back then lads our homes to share.

Boys
No ! by the bar tree blossom ! but
You come with us and share our hut.

Girls
The birds sing merrily, we agree
To leave pa ma and go with thee.

(Bhuiyas—Assam and Bihar).

The visit is soon returned by the girls. They are received by the young men in their *darbar* and entertained, and the girls of the receiving village must not be seen. However, they appear to have very great liberty, and slips of morality, so long as they are confined to the tribe, are not much heeded. Their songs have certainly more wit, more romance, and more poetry in their compositions than is usually found amongst the country folk in India.

Bihu Songs

The Magh and Baisakh Bihus are the great festivals of the Assamese. The observances connected with these festivals have nothing to do with the Hindu religion, and their origin is involved in some obscurity. The Baisakh - Bihu is a festival of spring and the hearts as gay as a carnival, and whilst it lasts, the women, especially the maidens, enjoy unusual liberty. For many days before the actual festival, the young people in the villages may be seen moving about in groups gaily dressed or forming circles, in the midst of which the prettiest girls dance with their long hair loose on their shoulders. The first day of the festival is devoted to interchanges of visits, the next to the bathing and worshipping of all cattles, and on the third day the inhabitants of several groups of villages, old and young, meet at some appointed place and give themselves up to thorough enjoyment. Lovers take the opportunity of this seasonal joy to express their hearts to their beloved. The theme of the Bihu song is mostly romance and love. Here are a few specimen :

You hated me when I was young
Because of my nasty nose
You appreciate me now
Seeing the beautiful beads in my neck.
Husk the paddy
Throw away the hay
Forget me and my love
So that my parents may not know.
I shall leave my mother
I shall leave my father
I shall leave my brother too,
Better die taking poison
I cannot live
without your love and you.

(Karbis—Assam)

Among the Darrang Kacharis, the April Bihu seems to be a 'Saturnalia' of much more objectionable character; the people abandon themselves freely both to drunkenness and licentiousness. During the festival lasting for seven days amid feasting and sheer merriment, the younger folks especially rejoice themselves dancing and singing. The verses sung at these festivals seem mostly a little better than mere meaningless jingle-jangle rhymes made up on the spur of the moment.

The following three couplets, freely translated, give an insight into the cheerful, festive mood of Kachari family members (brother and sister), their exchange of playful banter, and excitement to hurriedly put on finery with the best sari to embellish oneself before going out for celebration; their joy and rustling sound of the clothes, as though heard, are so vivid to the temperament of the occasion.

Sister Boisagi, come out and play;
This is our Bihu holiday;
Don't move inside the house all day.

Dear brother mine, I'll come anon
I'm putting my best sari on ;
Five minutes' grace; don't harshly press;
we ladies *must* have time to dress.

Uncle's a wealthy *mauzadar*,
Long has he served the great Sirkar;
He'll gladly give a bounteous feast,
Around half-dozen pigs at feast.

(Kachari—Assam)

The brother, with all young man's impatience and eagerness to enjoy the fun, calls his sister, Boisagi, to come out from the house and join him at once, while she from within pleads woman-like for a few minutes longer grace to complete her adornment. Both brother and sister assure themselves that their nearest relative, a *mauzadar*, would provide ways and means for a plentiful Bihu feast.

The groups of Miris in the plains are to be found amongst the gayest of the revellers in these days. The Miri damsels, the village belles, dance the somewhat sensual Bihu dance with great spirit. Their Lingang festival is similar to that of Bihu during which the adult unmarried males and females of a village spend several days and nights together in one large building, and if couples manage thus to suit each other, they pair off and marry. Their folk song Kalicipad (which they claim to be the oldest form) mostly give expression to their sentiments of love and yearning. Free rendering of a popular Miri Bihu song enjoyed by them is given below :

I would be a bird and wing to your lake,
I would be a pigeon and flutter on your roof,

I would be perspiration and well up in your body,
I would be a fly and fall on your cheek.

(Miris—Arunachal Pradesh)

Yearning and bird motif is very common in the Miri folk songs.

Some specimen of English translation of Bihu songs (taken from folk-literature of Assam by Praphulla Datta Goswami) are given below. Feeling disturbed, the girl sometimes sings in anguish :

What have I eaten up O - mother O father
that you babble about me
only let this year's Bihu be over, my father
not long shall I stay in your house

This yellow bird, lovely its wings,
once it flies up, it cannot be caught,
this youth, if it goes away
no more is to be got back.

Looking at the girl walking on the meadow and infatuated by her carriage, her lover sings :

High you tied your long hair,
as you tied your long hair,
as you walked, you crushed the grass
as I looked into your eyes you smiled,
wild you made my mind.

In mirth and gibe, the young married woman makes a ribald-humour at her brother-in-law:

I throw at the mango
why does the tamarind fall,
as brother-in-law, I offer him a seat
how is it he snatches at my breast.

(Assamese—Assam)

Love and Pathos

The origin of the Thadous of Manipur is shrouded in obscurity. However, the opinion goes that the Chins of Burma, the Lushais and Thadous are of the same stock, but the inter-tribe feud, subsistence resource-crunch and increase of population forced them to migrate and undergo twin process of assimilation and isolation, bringing thereby a change in their racial composition. Their musical instruments are common with the Chinese ones, and their language falls within the Kuki-Chin group of the Tibeto-Burman family. The word Thadou itself is a Burmese word meaning courage. As a result of a mythical flood, the Thadous took refuge at Kholkipkholjang located in Manipur to the right bank of Imphal river.

The biggest preoccupation of a Thadou boy is the quest for a girl. His aesthetic appreciation of her beauty, deep sense of mutual love and promotion of inter-tribe friendship are the main objectives behind their nuptial knots. Here, the story of Ngambon and Khupting is relevant. Ngambom loved Khupting, and wanted to marry her. The girl's family refused because the elder sister of Khupting was still unmarried. Ngambom created a clay-image of her and kept it by the side of Imphal river and used to visit it daily. One day it was carried away by the river. Ngambom could not trace it. Incidentally Khupting also died:

> "I followed the length of river
> the long river I followed
> I could not trace Tingo (Khupting's nick name)"
>
> (Thadous—Manipur)

The endless wandering and eternal quest followed by dark despair are expressed in as few words as possible through the powerful imagery.

"Tired, sitting in the stage of the world, then hast taken in the immortal world. Oh : my dearest be kind to come,

For our enemies are come and go ahead"

(Maiteis—Manipur)

The lover on finding the death of his beloved caused by mental agony and disturbances pronounced that their love will be immortal. He addresses her to come out of the miseries and imperfections of the world and appear in front of him. He expresses his desire to establish an ideal society which is above sorrow and limitations. This song is also sung at the time of the funeral procession and makes a heart-rending impression on the social life of the people.

The Miris of the plains keep much to themselves, leading rather a nomadic life living in houses on stilts built on the precarious banks of the Brahmaputra and its estuaries or effluents, and cultivating on the alluvial flats of the river. The young women crop their hair and attach to the cropped ends an ornament—fringe of cowries and brass beads, which give them the appearance of wearing a wig in a very fantastic manner. They wear a small petticoat made of filaments of cane woven together. It is about a foot in breadth, and fastened so tight round the loins and worn like a Sarong that it restrains free movement of the thighs, and causes the women to move with a short mincing motion chiefly from the knee. The women, like their Konyak counterparts, are often seen with nothing on except this singular garment. They have the deep tenor voice and slow method of speaking.

It is worth noting that they have a kind of sorrowful songs known as Ai-nitam songs. These songs, although on love-theme, depict their deep longing for the beloved and sense of frustration and sadness due to love failure:

If I do not secure you here
I shall secure you in the next world
Where is Yama's city
there, I shall meet you.

If fate does mean our union,
then, after death,
he shall grow to grasses in the cemetry,
and put us together.

(Miris/Mishings—Arunachal Pradesh)

Here, deep frustration seeks solace in union after death. Bidhi (destiny), Bidhata (God, fate), Kapal (Kamphal, forehead, writing on forehead, fate), Yama (Yamraja, God of death), dos (blame, error) etc. find copious expression in Ai-nitam songs.

The Miris managed to serve themselves as medium of communication between Assamese and Abors, and they obtained this name Miri, which means mediator or go-between; it is the same word as 'miria' or 'milia' used with the same signification as in Orissa. Perhaps, the meriah applied to the sacrifice of the Khunds is a cognate word, the meriah being the messenger or mediator between man and the deity. Some of the copious expressions cited above are derivatives of the Assamese.

Miris being the medium as described here, a word on the resemblance their women bear in their dress with the Abors requires a mention here.

The dress of the Abor females as ordinarily seen consists of two clothes, blue and red in broad stripes. One round the loins forms a petticoat just reaching to the knees, it is tied in its position by a girdle of cane-work; the other is folded round the bosom, but this is often dispensed with, and the exposure of the person above the waist is evidently considered no indecency. Their necks are profusely decorated with strings of beads reaching to the waist, and the lobes of the ears are, as usual with the hill races, enormously distended for decorative purposes. Round the anklets, so as to set off to the best advantage the fine swell of the bare leg, broad bands of very finely plaited cane-work are tightly laced; some of the belles, very particular about their personal appearance, wear these anklets of a light blue tinge. But the most singular article of their attire remains to be described. All females with pretensions of youth wear round their waist a row from three to a dozen shell-shaped embossed plates of belt-metal, suspended in front from a string. These plates are about six to three inches in diameter, the largest in the middle, the others graded in diminishing size as they approach the hips. These plates rattle and chink as the women move, like prisoners' chains.

Very young girls, except for minimum of clothing to keep themselves warm, wear nothing but these appendages, and even adult females are often seen with no other coverings. While dancing, they divest themselves of everything else, and behave in a very indecorous manner which bears a striking similarity with the sensual dance of the Miri girls during Bihu.

The total exposure of their persons by certain hill tribes denuding all coverings seems to have a direct bearing on the physical attraction they command, the love-life and sexual freedom they enjoy while courting with their mates. Nevertheless, they are not free from the sardonic pathos emanating from the frustrating affairs caused by some social restraints which prohibit not only the marital unions but also premarital love-making among the members of the community. The Abors view with abhorrence the idea of their girls marrying out of their own clan. When one of the daughters of Padam demeans herself, a belief is privalent that the sun and the moon will refuse to shine, and there is such a strife in the elements that all labor is necessarily suspended, till with sacrifice and oblation the stains are washed away.

This reminds one of the system of morung and clan exogamy among Konyaks, which if observed so long, no one interfered with the amorous adventures and complete sexual freedom among young people. Of all the people in the North East of India, the Konyaks are considered in many ways the physically most attractive, having slender built and delicate structure. Both men and women took a great deal of trouble over their appearance and sported numerous colourful ornaments; their black hair well combed, often with a fresh flower stuck in earlobe or hair knot.

In the older literature, the Konyaks were sometimes referred to as "naked Nagas", and in the recent past this description was still justified. Occasionally, girls with developed breasts and pubic hair could be seen walking nude in the village, but adult women put on a narrow oblong piece of cloth wrapped round the waist, with one corner tucked in over the left hip, just enough to cover the private parts, while men and youths seldom wore more than a tight belt and a loin cloth. Many middle-aged men worked naked in the house and field. The custom of covering the private parts was probably of comparatively a recent origin.

The passionate love-affairs, gratification of emotional urges and indulgence in promiscuity by boys and girls and even by the young married couples involved no obligations on either side. However, the pathos is well-wrought even within this overall framework granting considerable latitude. As soon as the young love became pregnant, she would have to enter her legitimate husband's house and live in his house. The child born would be recognised as that of the woman's legitimate husband. It so happened that several children of a person would be growing in other men's houses, while his wife's children, who were that of another man grew up in his house as his own.

Personal tragedy is imminent on any of the established spouses committing adultery in extramarital escapades which are considered to be the moral turpitude as in our civilised society today.

With a view to bring the pathos under minor scrutiny, a further look into the system of exogamy is necessary. In Konyak village, for a young boy the girls of his own village fall within two classes : potential mates with whom he may flirt and joke, and the girls of his own *morung* or *morung* group, whom he has to treat like sisters and in whose presence he is not to mention any sexual matters. The daily contact with a large number of attractive young girls, ever present in the village and yet placed out of reach by the strongest of taboos, would give rise to many a secret and hopeless romance. The blind adventures with such 'forbidden' girls are perhaps thrusted as reaction out of the unconscious realm of the young Konyak to this system, and there can be no doubt that incest, although one of the most serious social crimes, is not without romantic associations. The incestuous love of a brother and sister—standing here perhaps for any couple thwarted in love by the rules of exogamy - is the subject of a short, terse song, rendered below:

Yinglong and Liwang
Dearly loved each other.
Loving they lay together
Red as the leaf of the *ou-bou* tree,
Flamed love and desire.
On the paths to the village,
The two lit fires,
Skywards, upwards curling,
The smoke of the fires united,
and mingled, never to part.

(Konyak—Nagaland)

"In this poem the love of Yinglong and her brother Liwang is not condemned but idealized," observes Haimendorf. Of course, concrete instances of brother-sister incest could hardly have occurred, or at least not came to light, a passion so unorthodox and the tragic plight of the unfated lovers have been found transformed into happy fulfilment of a union into the people's romantic imagination which reveals the lofty temperament of hedonistic folk culture engrossed in love and carnal desires.

Similar taboo was also prevalent among the Aos which was later on dispensed with when a supernatural manifestation believed to have taken place on the death of a young couple in love who were denied marriage by their respective parents of two different groups, the Chongli and Mongsan. However, there are myriad reasons for the lover's boat finding no smooth sailing where there is rocky course to flounder in the world of loveless ethos. Jiṇa, a young man, and Etiben, one of the most beautiful girls of her time, were in deep love but their love affair was vitiated by the parents of Etiben not granting consent to their marriage. When Etiben fell seriously ill and was about to die, she sings:

> Beloved, oh, I am about to die,
> In this world though not married,
> In the far away lower land to marry
> Darling, will you come not – ?

The girl had no hope for her intense desire to marry or for panacea of her serious illness she is suffering from. She knows that she is doomed forever. Nevertheless, as a solace she asks the boy whether he would be willing to follow her to marry unto the nether world believed by Aos to exist underneath the world.

> Jina responds :
> Why not come,
> You precious, my beauty,
> Please wait unmarried.

> Etiben replies :
> Beloved, of us, whoever first depart,
> The last one, in the grave of first depart,
> Should drive flies,
> Wrapping shawl from left side
> On the tomb flower be placed.

(Ao—Nagaland)

Her last wishes are that amongst the two lovers, whoever is survived should drive away the flies from the deceased body and wrap up a shawl from the left side to bemoan while placing a wreath on the grave.

In an Angami folk song, the excruciating pain resulting out of the violent death of a beloved at the hands of her lover done inadvertently is so subdued that the tragic event stands as a matter of fact, as an ordinary occurrence in the course of life. No bewailing and crying—rather the mundane affairs. The experience at the end is that of Aristotelian catharsis of emotions when the girl makes modest entreaty to the boy to visit her grave every day during the five days of "dead genna period" and to take out the axe from her body.

Our village observes thikesa,
No going to field but all at home,
Take my adze at hand, axe on shoulder.
There to the jungle walk proudly,
There a branch of tree way nearby.
That, to take to make,
The handle of my lover's hoe.

But God changed my plan.
My axe comes out and penetrates her.
I catch a wild fowl secretly,
Take this and recover soon.
This may be taken but recover not, darling;
Visit my grave within all five days,
And take out your axe please.

(Angami—Nagaland)

Marriage

As stated above, in tribal society the promiscuity involved not much obligations on either side, but if two young people had been lovers for some time and had become fond of each other, they began to consider marriage. Usually, it was the boy who took the initiative and asked the girl whether she was willing to become his wife. If a girl did not relish the prospect of marrying her lover or feared opposition from her parents, she would refuse his proposal and shelter behind the authority of her parents. Although parents sometimes arranged marriage, an attempt to forbid their unmarried daughter a friendship with a particular boy would have aroused general disapproval. Moreover, at some places the institutions like girls' dormitories, *Dhangarin bassa,* or *Mandarghar,* and house for maidens, which strangely, they are allowed to occupy without anyone to look after them, have made parental control impracticable. In such cases, it was generally accepted that a girl would have sexual relations before marriage. Virginity was neither valued nor expected of a young girl there. A girl, determined to hold on to her lover, could usually get her way, or, as a last resort, elope with him to a friendly village.

In olden times young men counteracted the machinations of avaricious parents against the course of true love by forcibly carrying off the girl. Then the parents had to submit to such terms as arbitrators think fair; and on payment of the usual bride-price, at a somewhat enhanced rate, the parents raised no further objection to their daughter's union with the abductor. Now, 'marriage by capture' is rapidly becoming out of vogue, if indeed be not already absolutely a thing of the past; otherwise the marriage contract was usually entered into by the parents on mutual settlements paying stipulated price of the prospective bride or her estimated value in cows, pigs, fowls, or drink; those who were too poor to pay in cash served like Jacob in her father's house till they have given an equivalent in labour as has been practised among Kirantis. From this resulted in a few instances, the practice of polyandry amongst poorer groups of near about Tema's tribe who were required to work hard to earn the means of buying a wife. On the other hand, polygamy is practised to a great extent by the chiefs of Panibotia Miris, the Temas, Hos, Mishmis, Subanshiri, Abors, Manipuris and Konyaks; there is no limit, but his means of purchase, to the number of wives a man may possess, and (as amongst the Mishmis) when he dies, his son or heir will become the husband of all the women, excepting his mother.

The Padams have contempt for such a plurality and

generally repudiated the custom; as leading to jars and dissensions. Fathers and mothers have little occasion to "manoeuvre" matches of their children and they seldom interfere; and to barter their child's happiness for money would be regarded as an indelible disgrace.

It is certainly not from any yearning for celibacy that the marriage of Singbhum Ho maidens is long postponed. The girls will tell you frankly that they do all they can to please the young men, sometimes even pathetically bewailing their want of success. They make themselves as attractive as they can, flirt in the most demonstrative manner, and are not too coy to receive in public attentions from those they admire. They may be often seen in well assorted pairs returning from market with arms interlaced, and looking at each other as lovingly as if they were so many groups of Cupids and Psyches, but with all this the *"men will not propose"*.

Tell a maiden you think her nice looking, she is sure to reply "Oh yes ! I am, but what is the use of it, the young men of my acquaintance don't see it." Even when a youth has fully made up his mind to marry, it may happen that the fate is against the happiness of the young couple; bad omens are often seen as the cause for the match to be postponed or broken off, or papa cannot, or will not, pay the price demanded by girl's father. When the terrible question of the 'pan' (price of the bride) discussed, many matches are broken off, in consequence of greediness on one side or stinginess on the other. Therefore, in this part of India many spinsters are found so advanced in years, and in many of the best families grey headed old maids may be seen, whose charms were insufficient to warrant the large addition to the usual price called 'pan', imposed in consideration of the high connection that the union would confer. The 'pan' is calculated, and for the most part paid, in cattle, indicating that the custom dates from a time when there was no currency notes or coins, and fathers of Manki dignity demand from forty to fifty heads of cattle for each of their girls. The amount agreed on has to be paid before the day can be fixed for the marriage, and when the delivery of the cattle is made, a pot of beer has to be given from the bride's side for each animal.

At last, if all this is got over, the appointed day arrives, and the bride is escorted to the village of her intended bridegroom by all her own young female friends with music and dancing. The young men and girls of the village, and those invited from neighbouring villages, form a cortege for the bridegroom. They go out and meet the bride's party, and after a dance in the grove, in which the bride and bridegroom take part, mounted on the hips of two of their female friends, they enter the village together, where there is a great feast, a great consumption of the rice bear, and much more dancing and singing. Ceremony there is none, but the turning point in the rite is when the bride and groom pledge to each other a cup of beer is given to each; the groom pours some of the contents of his cup into the bride's cup, and she returns the compliment. Drinking the liquor thus blended, they become of one 'Kili', that is, the bride is admitted into her husband's tribe, and they become one. This has succeeded an older custom of drinking from the same cup.

> "The bride touched the goblet, the knight took it up,
> He drank off the wine, and he threw down the cup."

After remaining with her husband for three days only, it is the correct thing for the wife to run away from him, and tell all her friends that she loves him not, and will see him no more. This is, perhaps, reparation to the dignity of the sex injured by the bride's going to the bridegroom's house to be married, instead of being sought for and taken as a wife from her own. So it is correct for the husband to show great anxiety for the loss of his wife and diligently to seek her, and when he finds her, he carries her off by main force. Sometimes, a young wife thus found and claimed and borne away, can be seen screeching and struggling in the arms of her husband, in the midst of a crowded bazaar.

No one interferes on these occasions, and no one assists. If the husband cannot manage the business himself, he must leave her alone.

After this little escapade, the wife at once settles down, assumes her place as the well contented mistress of the household, and as a rule, in no country in the world are wives better treated. A Kol or Ho makes a regular companion of his wife. The unfaithful wife is discarded, and the seducer must pay to the husband the entire value of the 'pan'.

Owing to the high price placed on daughters by their fathers, the large number of adult unmarried girls, seen in every considerable village in the Kolhan, is a very peculiar feature of the social state of the community. As a consequence of such practice, the number of marriages has been diminishing annually and immoral intimacy between the sexes increasing. Barring these few tribes, generally the young people arrange their matrimonial affairs themselves and a feast followed by some convivialities is the only ceremony required to ratify and declare the happy event; but it is customary for a lover to show his inclinations whilst courting by presenting his sweet heart and her parents with such delicacies and valuables as per his means, as a gory token of his love.

So far selection of partners is concerned, the Bhuiyas have a marvellous, pretty and romantic fashion of bringing about such matches, the only difference from the rest of the tribes in the North East being that the proposal of marriage comes in the first place from the girl, as with the Garos. On the topic of marriage, the pledged lovers, after free indulgence of passions during their love-play at night together, sing the songs of extempore compositions. There is a leader on each side of the groups of young men and damsels who starts with some word or name or phrase introduced chiefly for the sake of the rhyme, but generally opposite to the idea that follows, somewhat in the style of that classical fragment of didactic poetry—

Blankets and pins ! blankets and pins !
When a man marries his sorrow begins.

There is, no doubt, an intentional connection between the first and the second line. Blankets are suggestive of warmth and comfort which may be associated with fortunate matrimony, but blankets with pins in them are horribly expressive of the misery of ill-assorted unions. The mirth-loving, hilarious and witty character of the Bhuiyas is revealed precisely through these two terse stanzas only.

The proposal from a young man for marriage scrutinised by the girl ultimately leads to rejection in their dialogues as stated below :

Girl : How have you built the walls of your house?
Boy : Walls have been built with lamado worth ruppees hundred.
Girl : Of what is the roof built ?
Boy : Roof has been built of big 'tal', i.e. Kasi (cymbal), worth of two thousand rupees.
Girl : What are the materials with which the house has been tied?
Boy : The ropes are made from silver (i.e. murkonats).
Girl : How are the poles ?
Boy : The poles are made of gold (i.e., en)
Girl : How is the hearth ?
Boy : That has been built with three costly bells (i.e. deoghanti worth hundred rupees.)
Girl : You do not have much wealth and good house. I can consider your proposal for marriage if you can uproot the biggest tree onthe other side of the hill and plant just here, or if you can catch a white crocodil from the river, or if you can catch alive the wild white bear from the forest by whatever magical power (that you may have). Otherwise, whatever may be the

amount of wealth you may have, I will not agree to your proposal.

(Hillmiri—Arunachal Pradesh)

It is observed in the song that neither the women are subjugated in these societies nor any decisions by the male-folks are imposed upon them.

Biyar git or the songs pertaining to the marriage ceremony of the Bengalee Hindus occupy a unique position among the folk songs of the Cachar district. These beautiful songs are sung on the days on which the *Mangalacharan, adhibas, kanya biday* (giving send-off to the bride) rites are observed. It is in the late hours of the night when performing *adhibas* that these songs are sung in large number. The wedding takes place on the following night. The night of the *adhibas* has been compared with the night of the ninth day of the lunar fortnight of the Bengali month of Aswin (*nabami-nisi)*. The bride's mother is full of anxiety whether her daughter will be able to adjust with the members of the family of her husband and the husband himself. The mother has fulfilled her many childish demands and tolerated many of her annoying childish acts. But will her daughter's mother-in-law also show the same loving tolerance towards her daughter-in-law ? The help-lessness of a newly-wed girl in the family of her husband is depicted very beautifully in the song, the text of which is quoted below:

Oh my sweet daughter,
    put on the ornaments of gold
Put them on sitting alone,
    though you are still a suckling.
At your mother's house,
    you would refuse the dish of milk and banana
Even on repeated insistence.
    In an alien's household
None is likely to insist you.
    In your mother's house you used to waste
Rice around and fish your whole dish

Will the mother of anybody else tolerate this ?
Oh my dearest daughter,
That somebody else's mother will speak ill of you
Your heart will not be able to bear;
(In such an event) tears will roll down your eyes ;
Oh, how will you put up with the moment
When (they) will drag the names of your father,
Mother and brother and call them names ?
Oh my dear daughter, I prayed to
and had boons from all the gods,
And (then) gave you in marriage, my sweet daughter
May Sulapani keep you happy and well.

(Bengalee—Assam)

The songs which have been composed on this heart-rending pain of separation are the songs possessing the highest literary quality and expressing the innermost human feelings and emotions. How will the bride's mother console herself when her daughter goes away from her care ?

"Seeing off my dearest daughter,
How shall I be able to pacify my heart,
(And) how shall I live here alone ?
Smear your feet with sandal paste
And put and leave your foot-prints (on a paper etc.)
Looking at which I shall be able to pacify my mind".

(Bengalee—Assam)

While sending her daughter off, the mother remembers things and events of the past. She remembers also how great sufferings she had to undergo to bear the child :

"For twelve years I kept my ritual vow,
And ate with the left hand

And it is by observing this rite
That I got you."

(Bengalee—Assam)

The loom is considered to be as precious to the Assamese maiden as life itself. There is a folk-song which says that the loom also wept along with the members of the family on hearing the settlement of marriage of the daughter :

"Bargharat Kandile make bapeke
Moralat Kandile bhani
Bari pisefale Kande tatar shale
Aideuk bia dibar shoni."

(Assamese)

(On hearing the finalisation of marriage of the damsel of the house, parents started weeping in the dwelling house and the younger sister wept in the marriage pandal, while the loom wept behind the dwelling house.)

The Assamese people and Bangladeshis from the Sylhet district of Eastern Bengal have 'Baramahi' songs with imaginative contents moving on two parallel backgrounds—the super-structural background of religion on the one hand, and the economic background on the other. Lack of enthusiasm for marriage bears testimony to the oppression of the people living under the inevitable economic situation of a growing mercantile civilization creating a crisis in the conservative and complacent feudal society. The characters of these songs are, therefore, in a miserable predicament of the conflict of the two social forces. Marriage, which is otherwise the most cheerful event of an agricultural community, is shunned in these songs either on religious and ritualistic ground cited in reference to the tragic story of Behula, a well-known mythical character of Hindu Purana, or on grim condition of economic grinding :

ashar maser din man barishan
garib huharir ghar binai kandan.

peto nai bhat keurar pinno nai tena
kanyar bari dito kita nijer ai jotena
darun beyaine-nu mano bujh na pay
amkablir lagiya putor bure khuchay

(Assamese)

(*Ashar* brings showers and tears to the poor mother-in-law. There is no food and no cloth. Let alone her obligation to give something to her married daughter, she does have nothing even for herself. But the mother of the son-in-law will not appreciate her problem and consequently her daughter will be tortured for not bringing wealth from home.)

In abject poverty, the oppressed class of people saw the marriage festivities of the rich in utter helplessness :

Jamaiya khani asle hay baro dhumdham
pabibari biya pare aite khaite dekhte aram.
hakkol akte khoya jay puyapuri saite.
bes kari dhali dey kaite na kaite

(Assamese)

(Bridegroom's arrival brings joyful atmosphere. It is a pleasure to behold a marriage celebrated in 'pabibari—bigman's house. It is a pleasure for you and your children to eat enough there.)

The composer, who must have been deeply involved in the collective emotion of the peasants, could present the reality in concrete images and successfully convey the general emotion of individual characters. He picked up the images and pictures from everyday life of the people, their social behaviour and sufferings. We get a glimpse of a developing complex society locked into a struggle with a hostile environment to which nature became a part, and its elements forming the objective correlation with the content of archaic imagination. The society had its complexities without being industrial and modern, and the people were aware of their struggle. But the awareness made them more helpless and miserable. Religion did not have an outgrowth to make itself separate from their material world of terrestrial life. The religious and spiritual phantasies and beliefs are shadowed by material images of economic life. This song is a social image of a particular community living in a particular region and in a particular period of history.

Social life

The folk songs, covering the journey of folk life beginning from the cradle and ending with the funeral, connote the spontaneous outburst of feelings, love, imagination, sentiments of the ancestors, morals and disciplines. Though sometimes predominantly religious, they mostly bear traces of other aspects discussed at length. Work song is a part of these aspects. Occupational songs such as weaving, wood cutting, boat making and rowing, fishing, etc., are not scanty. Even some of them are connected with the festivals and are philosophical in content. In course of time, in some places the work song has been changed into a kind of romantic song too in the form of snip-snap between the males and females or between two persons. This corresponds to the rural folk song performed by the villagers without the aid of any accompaniments like musical instruments. It is the result of the mutual influence of the cultures of the people of this part of the country, the heir to all the best that mankind has created.

Here no elaborate observation is made on the tribal folk songs comprising social life which are too many and cover many levels of activities. However, I am taking up a few different types of folk songs along with the socio-cultural expressions as manifest in them—songs concerning the works, domestic chores, Feast of Merit and communal gatherings, etc.

In Manipuri speaking areas, *Khunung Ishei* means song of the past. *Khulang Ishei* originally means the song at the time of help in work.

Here is a song sung while guarding corn fields against birds:

Ha Uri (tailor bird) the deaf
Thou dos't turn a deaf ear to thy mother's call
Thou dos't turn a deaf ear to thy father's call
Ya Ho Ho ya (sound to drive away the birds).

(Meitei—Manipur)

When the paddy ripened in the fields, this small bird destroyed the crops. The farmers who hoped to have a rich harvest of paddy found the crops all eaten up. They cried having lost their harvest and lamented for fear of resultant famine. The farmers made their bamboo platforms and grown up girls rhyme their tasks with the above song.

The following poem draws a succinct picture of the rural life of the Karbi woman and her surroundings wherein the calendarical time has no place. The toiling days have robbed her off her sense of the past and the future and both so much cummingled that she tries to count them on the teeth of the sickle, and the old age has struck upon her quite unawares. Despite this the tone of her narration is unusually sprightly.

I have harvested paddy in *Aghon*
    Broken the *nara* (green straw) under feet
I calculate the present and future
    In the teeth of the sickle
And count the stars in the sky.
    I have harvested paddy
In the month of *Aghon*
    With the crimson sickle in hand,
(I) need not invite sleep,
    It will come of its own.
You are beating the drum
    Oh brother.
Calling the dancing girl,
    Call her not
She will come of her own.
    From my childhood days
I reared cattle

The hair turned grey,
We shall not quarrel,
With love we should live and play.

(Karbis—Assam)

The fascinating sight of the golden paddy in the month of *Aghon* (November-December) is very much familiar to us. Similarly, the memory of childhood, the rearing of cattle in the fields and in jungles, and growing up amidst this environment leading a sturdy life adopts a didactic tone in the final stanza.

Praised by strangers ,
Path of the village of six thousand,
As if building royal street by forced labour,
Praise that good act.
Young boys and girls putting on new shawls,
Path where walk with romance,
Discomfort in my place came to the other land
And with longing saw the road makers.

The people of mighty village were engaged in annual clearance of a particular path when two women from a faraway village unknowingly happened to pass through the land. Both were on their way to sell the feathers of a Hornbill. This song was composed and sung in a moment of this danger. It was the custom of the village to slaughter any person passing that way on that particular day. The villagers captured these two women with the intention to slay. The two girls then outpoured their praises—"We, the strangers praise this path, where the inhabitants of a village numbering six thousand tread. Your labour is laudable since your work is just like construction of a royal road being carried out under the command of an almighty king, employing every person by force."

The second portion reveals—"The path is thronged by the young boys and girls of the village wearing new shawls. They walk on the path overjoyed relishing romance and rollicks.

"Having faced hardships in our place, we have travelled all along to this distant land for a piece of business and seeing those road makers, we were enthralled with longing."

Because of their affable posture and commending words, the amiable message had gone home, and these two women were freed. In alternation, some of the workers sang the song with amour exalting the two women;

The day of the village meeting,
The day of the young men road making,
Like birds two females,
Prevented from their journeys,
The leg tatoo shines on the new road,
Considering, your death is spared.

(Anonymous—Nagaland)

In traditional Naga life, its prominent feature is the giving of a grand sumptuous feast called Feast of Merit which reflects magnificence, elegance and lavish Naga way of life. After performing a series of ceremonies on grandiose scale in such feasts, a domestic animal Mithun is sacrificed. The villagers are regaled with wine and food, serving them rice and meat. The feast endows the donor with great honour and by virtue of this becoming a leading celebrity, he can wear special attires and ornaments ; he can adorn and beautify his house in special styles obtaining a high dignity and status in social life. Usually the Feast of Merit entailing honour and fame to the giver is thrown by the married man. Here is an Ao song sung at the sacrifical rite of the Mithun :

Looking at the Mithun,
Oh, my heart is breaking,
Oh apply not *dao* edge at the Mithun,
Slaughter it in proper way.

The grand Mithun, that brightens the village,
That highly precious Mithun,
Slaughter it in proper way.

In the premises of donor of merit- feast
Oh let me stay dancing,
Oh in the premises of donor of merit-feast
Let me dance, and be not sad.

(Aos—Nagaland)

The act of butchering the Mithun on the occasion of the Feast of Merit does not merely mean the brutal urge to demolish the animal nor it amounts to savagery. The song epitomises the intense pity swelling in the heart of a man at the sight of the Mithun being slaughtered. Seeing the plight of the Mithun, he is grief-stricken, overtaken by the heart-breaking pain. Therefore, he makes entreaty to the killers to be gentle while applying the sharp-edged *dao* rather than slashing it down with a direct stroke of cruelty. Of course, that majestic Mithun which is a glory to the village is fated to die. However, no fierce treatment be meted out to it. The narrator adds that he would rejoice in dancing while relishing the Feast of Merit in the house of its donor and would not be crestfallen at its killing.

Look, Oh ! Sangtams,
Crying the universe,
Ongngo the bird singing (and) singing human beings alike.
Voice of the universe, you and yourself heard or not?
Step forward, universe for you (everybody).
On your death die not universal tune ;
(Hesitate not) Think and feel for humanity.

(Sangtams—Nagaland)

The poem is laden with profound philosophical meaning. The poet is appalled to see his own people (community) in torpor and slothful condition. In the first two lines, he tries to arouse them from their inertia and hermetically closed world of isolation of bygone eras by pointing at the 'Universe crying' which signifies their lamentable way of life, as the people are apathetic to each other, out of hormony within themselves and lackadaisical. Theirs is the life led against the law of nature, not in tune with the humanity as a whole spreading all over the world. At the same time, it signals for them to rejuvenate their life by generating harmony and kinness with the rest of the human-race and every member of the human society.

The next line delineates the affinity between human race and the bird-animal world, the bird 'ongngo' standing as a representative of the nature. The bird singing evokes the simultaneous enchanting response from the human-heart which reciprocates with its sweet song, and thus both are emotionally attuned to each other.

The rest of the lines portray the all-pervasive, eternal voice of the universe beckoning the human-soul to listen to it. The poet asks : 'you and yourself heard or not ?' The summon is for taking 'a step forward' unitedly for prosperity of the humanity as a whole, since the world is for all, and not for a particular individual nor for his self-centred motive alone. He should, therefore, extend his hands for its all-round promotion and human upliftment; rather than while away his time in pettiness. The last two lines highlight the fact that though the man is perishable, his noble deeds done for the cause of service to the humanity are not, and he should not die this 'universal tune' along with his mortal self, but live immortal by his action and thought.

The above song is sung on communal gatherings and seldom on social festivities.

Grief, Brievement and Death

For centuries, the lands and the waters have not only supported but also protected the human life. At times, earthquakes and floods appeared to destroy crop and culture. But the destruction too had become an integral part of the basic cycle of creation. They, the people who made the North East region their habitat, learnt to live with their physical surroundings. The natural tides, both of fortune and misfortune, shaped the tribal minds and moulded their instincts to emerge in concord with the rivers and the mountains. This sublime unity of man with nature is splendidly reflected in their folk songs even while expressing their griefs and sorrows, their bereavement and portraying the theme of ultimate death.

Oh ! Father I searched for you about
In hunger and thirst
But found you not
In your dominion.
If you would give a hint
As to your dwelling place
I would know the tract
From the flowers and birds
And trees and creepers
To go there once.
They say you are omnipresent
The river, the hill, the sun and the birds say
That you lurk by everything,
But get you not.

I call you at the top of my voice
The dove and the myna
Laugh at me
Tell me Father, where you may be

(Bodo Kacharis—Assam)

This is a Bodo song sung by a daughter who is on an eternal search for her dead father. It has been seen that how her long lamentation reaches the rationalization that a person dead is never lost but remains alive in nature ubiquitously. The similar theme recurs in the following Nishi song :

Oh, old tree, do you know
Where my mother's sister has gone ?
Oh, big river, have you seen
My mother's sister ?

Oh, the tall hill,
Is my mother's sister here ?
Oh, where has she gone ?
I do not find you,
Oh, my mother's sister.
Have you taken the shape of a paddy plant,
And (thus) you are hiding (yourself) from us ?
I think it so, oh my mother's sister,
Let me take rest.

(Nishi—Arunachal Pradesh)

Here, a young man is in search of his mother's sister who, people say, is dead. He does not believe it and knocks the doors of the nature.

Ill-treatment of step-children by their step-mothers is universally revealed in the tribal folklore. Such circumstances are depicted in many folk songs and tales, thereby evoking the feelings of poignancy of tortured existence wherein the victims are subjected to utter deprivation and rendered to bemoaning the loss of the parents. They bewail their orphaned condition. A Sema step-son used to sing :

Wolo Wolono
Being an orphan, being an orphan,
Hot rice served to real son,
Cold rice being my share.
Hot tea served to a real son,
Cold tea being my share.

What to do ?
Being an orphan, being an orphan,
I do countless work,
But it is nothing in the eyes of my master,
With my grief,
Crying on my father's grave.

Hey ! my father, hey ! my father,
Where have you gone ?

Hey ! mummy where are you ?
Hey ! mummy where are you ?
It is the living worry of an orphan,
Zulo Zulono.

(Sema—Nagaland)

Lastly, the free translation of a Chakhesang song, describing the longing of an old native for his youth and his distress over the impending onslaught by the fatality of fate, is given below:

Born pure and innocent like a flower,
With the blessings of my parents, my dear parents,
My life was planned to be as ever flowing as a stream,
And as peaceful and glorious as a blooming rose.

As a child, I had no cares no worries no fear,
Nor did I ever dreamt of a thing such as death.
I spent my youth with joy and happiness,
Never I felt sorrow in my heart.

Full of joy, gaiety and laughter,
Everything and everyone around me was cheerful and bright.
It seemed the whole world was made for me
To give me pleasure.

But, alas ! as the years rolled by,
And as I grew in age and wisdom,
I began to realise life on this earth,
Is not eternal, not for ever, not everlasting.

I learn life is short-lived,
The treasures, the glories and the sorrows,
One day would fade and die,
I find death an inescapable thing

Our lives are not like the roses,
That wither and fade today,

Their beauty will once more be seen,
In the next spring time.

Today the sun will set, the moon disappear,
Tomorrow they will be there shining,
As unchanged as ever in all their immortal glory.
But once we die, the beauty, joy, fear and sorrow
end.

With death we have no more,
The joys, sorrows, happiness and fear,
But only peace, everlasting peace.

Recalling the days of my youth,
I could see and understand how life has changed,
What a mystery and how strange death is.
Before we meet our eternal fate,
Let us one and all join hands together,
For death shows no distinction,
To rich and poor, young and old.

(Chakhesang—Nagaland)

At a cursory glance, it will be observed that the stylistics of a large number of these poetries are characterised mostly by predominance of images; the poets communicate with the audience through imagery rather than plain statements. Powerful images are created sometimes not only to impress the listeners, but also to express the extraordinary ancestral mores by allusions and implications. Allusion is found even when one word or expression which calls to one's mind some well-known past incident especially while using metonymy. Generally, the lines are extremely concise and compact; most of the matter is expressed in a as few words as possible. The concentration gives strength and dignity to the lines, where there is no room for connective words. The word 'and' seldom occurs in such traditional poetries, though other conjunctions are sparingly used.

Wherever the poetries are in rhymed couplets, all lines are end-straped. The lines of the couplets are complementary, and a unit of sense is complete at the end of a couplet. At times, the lines are also characterised by frequent use of alliteration, assonance and onomatopoeia and loaded with figures of speech which add to their beauty. It is an elevated style *par excellence* and inimitable for those who are not accustomed and grown up with it.

Some of the poetries are allegorical. Human life is allegorically described blending the elements of fables and parables. Pungent sayings are easily adopted and subsumed in epigramatic form. Hyperbole or exaggerated statements are made when things are presented as greater or lesser, or word them as they really are. In the use of antithesis, contrasted words or ideas are set against each other in a balanced form for strengthening the idea. All these features lend power and dignity to the verse qualities which are, more or less, similar to the written poetry of the literate period.

References

1. Hudson, J.H., The Meitheis, London, David Nutt, 1908.
2. Marak , L.R., Dikki - I, Shillong.
3. Hutton, J.H., The Sema Nagas (with a foreward by Henry Balfur), London, MacMillan, 1921; 2nd edn. Bombay Oxford University Press,1969.
4. Kumar, Dr. B.B., Folklore and Folklore Motifs, New Delhi, Omson's Publications, 1993.
5. Furer - Haimendorf Christoph VON, Return of the Naked Nagas, New Delhi, Vikas Publishing House, reprint, 1976.
6. ———, The Konyak Nagas, London, Holt, Rinehart and Winston, 1968.
7. ———,The Role of songs in Konyak Culture, Man in India, 23 : 69-82, 1943—A collection and interpretation of Konyak songs.
8. Dalton, Edward Tuite, Tribal History of India, New Delhi,Cosmo Publication, 1978.

9. Goswami, Prafulla Dutta, Folk Literature of Assam, Gauhati, 1965.
10. ———, Miri Folk Songs, IFL, II : 2, 1959 - Songs: Miri.
11. ———, Springtime Bihu of Assam, (A Socio-cultural study), Lawyers' Book Depot, Gauhati, 1966.
12. ———, The Bihu Songs of Assam, Lawyers' Book Stall, Gauhati, 1957.
13. ———, Kachari Ballads and Folk Songs, The Hindustan Standard, Oct. 14, 1945.
14. ———, Bohen Bihu of Assam and Bihu Songs, Assam Publication Board, Gauhati, 1988.
15. Munda, R. D., Cultural Elements in Ho Folk Songs, Calcutta, Indian Publications, 1971.
16. Mills, J.P., The Ao Naga (with a forward by Henry Balfour), London, Macmillan, 1926 ; Reprint, Bombay Oxford University Press, 1973.
17. Hutton, J.H., The Angami Nagas, 2nd edn. Bombay Oxford University Press, 1969.
18. Kirti Singh, Dr. M., Folk Culture of Manipur, Delhi, Manas Publication, 1993.
19. Endley, Rev. Sidney, The Kacharis, Delhi, Cosmo Publication,1975 (Reprint).
20. Joshi, Mahesh, Assam, The Indian Conflict, New Delhi, Prachi Prakashan, 1981.
21. Ao, Alemchiba, Arts and Crafts of Nagaland, Kohima, Naga Institute of Culture, 1968.
22. Marray, Parkes Colin, Bereavement : Studies in Grief in Adult Life, New York, Penguin, 1972.
23. Burton, Robert, Anatomy of Melancholy, 1961.
24. Barua, P.K., Kamrupiya Biya Geet (Marriage Songs of Kamrup), 1945.
25. Barakakati, Anand Devi, Biya nam (n.d.), Jorhat, 1948 - Assamese Songs.
26. Barua, Hamchandra, Marriage Customs of the People of Assam (n.d.) Gauhati, 1892.
27. Barua, T.K.M., Wancho Love Songs, Itanagar, Govt. of Arunachal Pradesh, Directorate of Research,1982.

28. Bhattacharya, P.C., Boro Songs on Love ; Indian-Folklore (II.I), 1957.
29. Brahma, Mohini Mohan, Folk Songs of the Bodos, Gauhati University, 1960.
30. Kalachand, Khamba Thoibi, Imphal, O.K. Store, 1963.
31. Roy, Sachin, Aspects of the Padam - Minyong Culture, Shillong, North East Frontier Agency, 1960.

Chapter 8

Folk Tunes

Tune - I

Tune - II

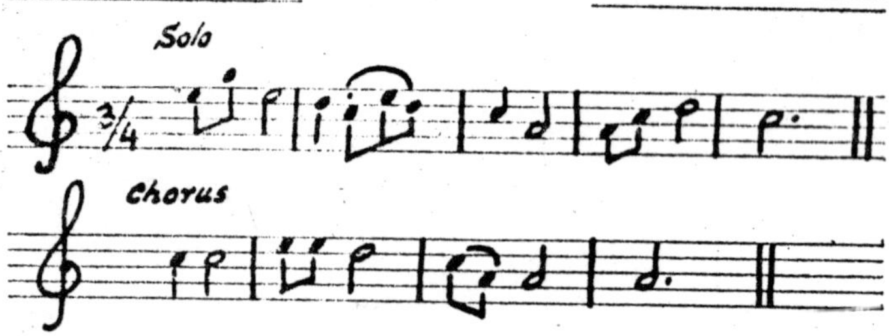

Tune - III

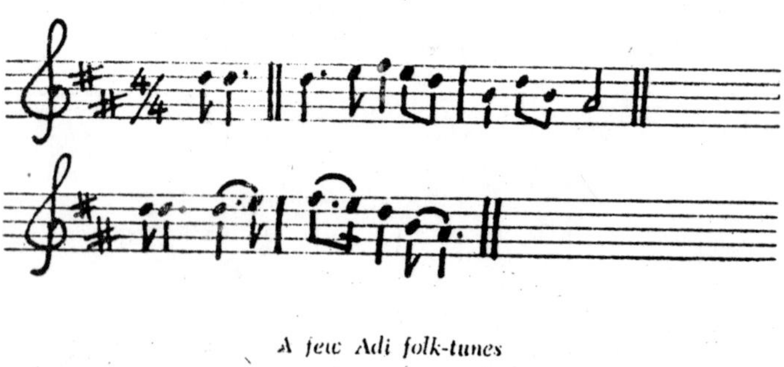

A few Adi folk-tunes

A few Adi folk-tunes

Chapter 9

Folklore Motifs and Interpretive Artistic Adaptation

IDENTIFICATION (SPECIAL REFERENCE TO THE NORTH-EAST OF INDIA)

My present disquisition will be incomplete if the core-subject of folklore i.e. its motifs is left unattended. It will be worthwhile to have identification of the folklore motifs and to see how its certain modes and motifs are subsumed by some of our modern literary forms, thereby rendering multi-dimensional interpretations to their artistic adaptation and thus nourishing and enriching the literary trends from our oral roots.

The motif is defined as "one of the dominant ideas in a work of literature ; a part of the main theme. It may consist of a character ; a recurrent image or a verbal pattern' in ' A Dictionary of Literary Terms.' In folklore, we quite often find thematic motifs where we have themes as motifs. The cruelty of step-mother is both theme and motif of a folktale. In the Jungian sense, the 'motif' is termed as such : "The concept of the archetype, which is an indispensable correlative of the idea of the collective unconscious, indicates the existence of definite forms in the psyche which seem to be present always and anywhere." Mythological research calls them 'motifs'.

Adolf Bastian called them 'primordial thoughts.'

Stith Thompson has published Motif Index of Folk-Literature (6 Volumes) in 1955-58 and has based his work on original works of A. Aarne. He wrote 'The type of the folktale' (1961) wherein 2499 folktale types are described. In the 'Types of Indic Oral tales ; India, Pakistan and Ceylon' by Stith Thompson and W.E.Roberts, we find proper oicotypes in the North East Indian folktales. Some important folk-motifs as per Thompsonian concept indexed in Thompson-Baley's Volume are extensively identified in the same form or with slight alterations in the North East Indian folklore. A gist of such motifs is given below :

1. Abduction of princesses and their rescues.
2. Angels/Animals/Birds/Deities as help in the service of man.
3. Abandonment (of various persons viz., abandoned/outcast wife, children and abandoned/orphan heroes).
4. Ascent to upper world/sky/heaven.
5. Alter-Ego.
6. Banishment.
7. Cruelty by step-mother/by others.
8. Curse.
9. Conception from casual contact between a maiden and moon and unearthly elements.
10. Disenchantments.
11. Deluge.
12. Double.
13. Deceptions/Dupings/Imitations etc.
14. False/Substituted wife.
15. Magic Objects/Rings etc.
16. Mysterious Persons/Elements etc.
17. Mutilation.
18. Punishments (for murder, cruelty etc.)
19. Prophecy and fulfilment.
20. Quest.
21. Reincarnations in plants/flowers etc.
22. Revenge.
23. Rewards for service to God/man/weak-orphans.

24. Recognition of son by gushing up of milk in mother's breast.
25. Resuscitation.
26. Scapegoats.
27. Seductions.
28. Secrets overheard/secret remedy overheard/secrets of animals (Demons) and secret knowledge of animal language.
29. Slander.
30. Tower of Babel.
31. Transformations (of various kinds).
32. Tabu looking back/beyond hillock/looking below.
33. Treachery (of various kinds) by various persons/relatives.
34. Talking animals/birds/plants etc.
35. Unequal marriages.
36. Victory.
37. Victims rescued.
38. Violations of Taboos and horror of incest.

INTERPRETIVE ARTISTIC ADAPTATION OF MODES AND MOTIFS

Now, it will be interesting to glance at the adaptation of the broad spectrum of modes and motifs of folklore by today's most popular and innovative literary form, the Short Story, practised by master craftsmen of the century. This will, most certainly,enlarge our perspectives in folkloristic research and its studies.

Throughout the past two centuries, the written tales particularly the short fiction, even more than the other forms of literature, has demonstrated its kinship with the oral narrative, and despite its various experimental masquerades—antistory, metafiction, surfiction—it gives no evidence of losing the ancestral likeness. In a great many of its thousand faces, lineaments of the folktale are readily discernible. If one has followed this Protean genre through its transformations to the point of its post-modernist trend, one might understandably start searching for resemblances between the tale of tradition and its brilliant sad sibling the modern short story, but the relationship remains, bend sinister or no.

In India, in Arab lands, in Italy, in China, and elsewhere there have flourished in earlier centuries short story traditions of much greater duration than our own "Era of 'The Overcoat'." The Indian *Jatakas,* stories about the many reincarnations of Buddha, began to appear in written text in the sixth century BC, and from the *Jatakas* grew a related but more secular form, the *Avadana,* creation of which continued well into the AD period. In the medieval Middle East the *Thousand and One Nights* was neither the first nor the last of the gatherings of tales written in Arabic ; from the same milieu came such other frame-story collections as *The History of the Forty Vezirs,* etc. There are scores of fine Italian *novellas,* notably those of Boccaccio, and an equally rich outpouring of Chinese stories by writers of the Ming Dynasty.

This literary form may well pride itself in being "heir of all the ages, in the foremost files of time"; like all heirs, it has its ancestors. Behind it extend many generations of forebears in the written tradition, and, still earlier, an almost endless line of progenitors in the oral tradition. Storytelling, it would seem, has been inherent to the human condition from the beginning. According to David Bynum, "storytelling is a peculiarly human activity. It is in fact a unique property of homo sapiens' societies." Although, in some ways the development of the genre during the "Era of 'The Overcoat' " has been a steady progression away from its oral matrix, in other ways the tale has never wandered far from home.

Though Poe's central dictum of his aesthetic of the written tale challenged the folktale tradition, for in most respects he remained closely attached to it and unwittingly paid silent tribute to the artistry that had fashioned thousands of tales before his time. His aesthetic was audience oriented : how to hold and captivate the attention of the reader. This he sought to do by pruning out discursive passages, unproductive digressions, interpolated stories, and the convolution of telescoping subplots. He was essentially distinguishing between the structure of the oral folktale and that of the printed literary tale. The art of the folk raconteur is highly effective in the oral context, where structure is not entirely predictable but develops en route according to the nature of the audience response. Here, the personality and the dramatic skill of the raconteur are also unifying elements of any oral performance. While, the writer, Poe seemed to be saying, must cleave doggedly to his forward course, affixing blinders to his eyes, as one does to the eyes of a horse, to prevent himself from being led astray by side glances from the straight and narrow path to his pre-established goal with unity of effect.

Despite his challenge to the folktale tradition, Poe retained the linear progression of the folktale, in fact emphasising it by his fixation upon the terminal effect. Most of his characters move in an ambience of romance rather than realism, and they themselves are, in general, static. As W.H. Auden has noted, his 'personages who are the embodiment of (unitary) states cannot, of course, change or vary in intensity either through changes in themselves or their environment.' Without much inner consciousness, they are stylized figures which expand into psychological archetypes.

The same might be said of most of the dramatis personae in the tales of his contemporaries Washington Irving and Nathaniel Hawthorne, though in such works as "My Kinsman, Major Malineux" and "Roger Malvin's Burial," Hawthorne did create characters who might, without too much adjustment, move into the modern short-story.

To come to the topic, the writers of the Romantic Period utilize not only the structure and characters of the folktale but also many of its themes and motifs. In Western literature, Irving's "Rip Van Winkle," "The Legend of Sleepy Hollow," "The Devil and Tom Walker," "The Spectre Bridegroom," and "The Adventure of the German Student" have analogues in Aarne and Thompson's *The Types of the Folktale*. Then, Hawthorne's "Ethan Brand," "Feathertop," "The Gray Champion," and his famous story "Young Goodman Brown" incorporate numerous elements listed in Thompson's *Motif-Index of Folk-Literature*. Even closer to the folktale are the short stories of a number of German writers of the late eighteenth and early nineteenth centuries : Novalis, Johann Ludwig Tieck, and E.T.A. Hoffmann. Their serious works are fairy tales for adults and not for little children.

Of course, a far bigger break with the tale of tradition came in the late nineteenth and early twentieth centuries with the stories of Chekhov and Conrad, Joyce and Lawrence, Mansfield and Hemingway, all of whom pursued in their respective ways the lead provided by Gogol, exploring the uncharted recesses of the internal landscape. With these writers the ending is no longer the be-all and the end-all, the locus of surprise or value judgement. The climax may well come in the middle of the story, occurring during a sudden and unexpected moment of revelation known as an *epiphany*. The structure is now not always linear, but is at points vertical. Chronology is scrambled, clocks no longer signallng the hour nor calendars the season ; instead, time is told by the psychic instruments of recall and association. Metaphor and symbol, point of view, and the reliability or unreliability of narrators grow in importance as authors strive to "create a fiction not of surface and clarity but of depth and complexity." Perhaps the most significant change takes place in the area of characterization, where the heroic mould has been broken and the protagonist is often the "little man:" Akakey Akakeivitch, the crushed copy-clerk in Gogol's "The Overcoat" ; Iona Potapov, the cabby in Chekhov's "The Lament" ; Maria, the pathetic charity case in Joyce's "Clay" ; or Miss Brill, the lonely fantasist in Mansfield's story of the same name. Dauntless heroes have given place to Thurberesque males and Chekhovian females, whether "chorus girls" or love-laden "darlings" or "ladies with pet dogs."

During our own time, the foundations of the tale of tradition seem to have suffered even further erosion. Plot has gone underground with no visible signposts for beginning, middle, and end. The chief structural element for providing unity or focus is no longer plot—and sometimes neither plot nor character—but theme. For example, Robert Coover's "The Babysitter" and Donald Barthelme's "To London and Rome," William Gas's "In the Heart of the Heart of the Country", John Updike's "The Music School" and Joyce Carol Oates' "How I Contemplated the World....." I do not mean to suggest that all of the stories of the '60s and '70s depend so heavily on theme via collage, but this technique is the common element in works by writers otherwise quite diverse. In such stories, climax is neither at the end, as it was in the tale of tradition, nor somewhere near the center, as it often was with the epiphanal story. Instead, it has been ground up and sprinkled evenly over the entire text to provide not a timely punch but a steady, slow pressure that builds into a cumulative effect of great force.

Whatever may be its transformations through all these ages till its post-modernist garb of much coveted content-orientation, the grip of folktale remains upon the short fiction. This statement may be easier to accept if one remembers that the word *folktale* is really an omnibus term, a broad rubric under which are subsumed several different modes; and, if one remembers, further, that each of these modes has its own purview and conventions. Largest of these oral modes is the *Marchen*, misnamed if one calls it the fairy tale. Here in are accounts of magics and marvels, of supernatural agencies which have no respect for those principles of cause and effect controlling the ordinary world. Childish, one might say, and quite unrelated to the concerns of serious fiction in an age dominated by science and technology ? Childish, perhaps, but relevant, nonetheless, to the extent that in our submerged and irrational inner selves we remain ever as children. The action of such narratives is informed by a species of psychological necessity. In 'A Sad Heart at the Supermarket' Randall Jarrell stated categorically, "...... the root of all stories is in Grimm, not in La Rochefoucauld ; in dreams, not in cameras and tape recorders". Jarrell was thinking of the psychic value of the *Marchen* for adult readers.

Naturally, the *Marchen* in modern literature appears in quite different semblance from what it did before in the Grimms' 'Household Tales' and it is often used as a means to a different end, but the basic tale remains. Admittedly, the modern writer must work harder to achieve in his reader "that willing suspension of disbelief for the moment which constitutes poetic faith," but the competent craftsman manages this. Since Henry James's publication of 'The Turn of the Screw' and 'The Jolly Corner', a long line of twentieth century authors have built successful stories on *Marchen* foundations. Familiar to most of our readers are E.M. Forster's "The Story of a Panic" and "The Story of the Siren," Joseph Conrad's "The Inn of the Three Witches," John Glasworthy's "The Apple Tree", D.H. Lawrence's "The Rocking-Horse Winner," Elizabeth Bowen's and Shirley Jackson's quite different stories with the same title, "The Demon (Daemon) Lover", Isak Dinesen's "The Sailor-Boy's Tale", and a number of Isaac Bashevis Singer's tales of the uncanny and occult set in the pre-World War II of Eastern Europe.

Closest to the *Marchen* stands the fable, a tale also involving the impossible or improbable but one which distinguishes itself by its didactic or moralistic purpose. Although allegorical in nature, most fables make patent the analogy between their characters and surface actions, on the one hand, and the qualities for which they stand, on the other. There have been relatively few beast fables of the Aesopic kind written in recent years, a fact that makes especially noticeable Orwell's "Animal Farm" and Thurber's *"Fables for Our Time"*. More common are stories cast in a fable-like atmosphere. Kafka's "A Country Doctor" and "In the Penal Colony" would fit into this classification, so would F.Scott Fitzgerald's "A Diamond as Big as the Ritz."

The legend differs from most folktales in that it is thought to be a true account of a historical figure or incident. Most of the material may be quite fictitious, but the legend adapts it from some remote factual origin and is given a specific, supposedly accurate, geographical setting plus quasi-historical documentation. Saints' legends are legion, and from two of them Flaubert and Unamuno fashioned successful short stories, "Saint Julian" and "Saint Manual the Good, Martyr," respectively. Inverting the formula, Steinbeck created the ironical and satirical "St. Katy the Virgin." Hawthorne used legend of New England in a number of his tales, such as "The Maypole of Merry Mount" and "Endicott and the Red Cross." Kafka's "The Great Wall of China" is in this mode, and so, quite clearly, is Udora Welty's "A Still Moment."

Even the tall tale–the yarn, as it is sometimes called–has its literary imitations, especially in the United States. Many people have produced tales of exaggerration, but nowhere else the mode flourished as it has in the United States. Of course, the scholarly studies of humour usually conclude that the native American strain is characterized by overstatement. Theirs is the land of big talk and oversize folk heroes. Mark Twain stands in the first row to have produced works filled with tall tales, or, as Huck Finn might have called them, "stretchers". Some of his stories retain folk qualities. Once past the frame and into the yarn itself, the reader is in no doubt about the mode. Faulkner frequently used the technique of the yarn in his comic stories, especially those featuring the escapades of the various members of the Snopes clan. The best known of these is undoubtedly "Spotted Horses," told by the most competent of Faulkner's colloquial voices, V.K. Ratliff, the semiliterate sewing machine salesman.

Among writers of the 1910s and 1920s Ring Lardner probably worked more than most of his contemporaries with the vernacular style demanded by the yarn. His most successful effort in the vernacular was a monologue called "Haircut." Although reflecting Lardner's usual irony, here developed by means of an insensitive and unreliable narrator, "Haircut" is a genuine yarn spun out at length by a garrulous barber in a typical small town. During the 1930s Stephen Vincent Benet may have been the artist who laboured hardest with this folk mode. Arthur Voss, in his history of the American Short Story, has described Benet's "The Devil and Daniel Webster" as "a tall tale which is one of the most famous of contemporary short stories."

If desired, one can demonstrate even more precisely the common ground shared by folktale and short story. If the modes in oral and written traditions are too comprehensive, possibly too loosely defined, to permit conclusive comparisons, then perhaps the smaller, more specific units will not be deemed so. An appreciable percentage of the plot patterns listed in Aarne and Thompson's index of folktale types, and of the persons, objects, and individual actions listed in Thompson's index of folk motifs can be shown to have been used by story writers of all time. The killing labour to redeem her son is the set for the peasant woman in Isak Dinesen's "Sorrow-Acre" parallels exactly folk motif H1010 – The Impossible Task. Thomas Mann's "The Transposed Heads" is a development of motif D 711.1.1 – Head Transferred from One Man to Another. (In Girish Karnad's drama '*Hayvadan*' the transfer of heads between two characters Kapil and Devdutta develops the similar motif). Robert Coover's "The Brother" like the Biblical story of Noah's Ark, is based on a motif especially common in the ancient Middle East, A1010 – The Deluge. Quite obvious are Hawthorne's uses of motif D1338.1.2 - The Water of Youth – in his "Dr. Heidegger's Experiment" and motif D 435 – Transformation, Image to Person (the Pygmalion motif) in his "Drowne's Wooden Image", and L.N. Andreyev's use of motif ED – Resuscitation – in his "Lazarus" for resurrection. To elaborate this correlation any further here would be tedious, but the literary use of such documentable folk elements has been drawing increasing attention from students and scholars both in literary as well as folkloristic studies.

The modes and motifs may bind together the folktale and the short story, but there is an even tighter tie between these two narrative traditions in their common capability as vehicle for myth. While one cannot, without reservation, equate folktale with myth, neither can one avoid the substantial available evidence indicating that most myth finds expression in narrative form. Whatever ritual origins myth may have had, in one place or another, whatever dramatization it may have been given, at one time or another, the individual myth usually involves the interaction of characters in a sequence of incidents which lead to the resolution of some problem. The myth of Prometheus or of Sisyphus or of Cupid and Psyche can hardly be understood on an abstract level until it has been envisioned on the concrete level (which has been treated in depth by me in chapter-3) as a progression of events in time. Thus, any given myth is likely to surface far more often in the shape of a tale than it is in any other guise. There are, for example, 533 folktale variants, in twenty-six languages of the Cupid and Psyche myth. Exactly how many variants there are among written tales is impossible to determine, for the short story has not, as yet, any reference work comparable to the Aarne-Thompson index of folktale types. Even John Barth has employed myth as a vital element in his art. And, conversely, myth – whether part of a belief system or, as it is frequently today, a time-tested parable – has found the short story peculiarly adaptable to its own esoteric ends. Because of its intensity, the short story engages the full attention of the reader, but because of its brevity, it does not ask the reader to suspend his disbelief too long.

To have pursued myth criticism of literature fifty years ago would have been to take a relatively short and uncomplicated trip ; to pursue it today is to follow a long, winding trail into the land of our dreams. Seemingly every writer (whether or not he knows it) is a mythologist, and every other critic a mythographer. However, even after discounting as mirage much of the quarry allegedly sighted by myth hunters, one must acknowledge that the field is still alive with the game. It takes no great effort or insight to recognize Christian myth in the stories of Hawthorne and Faulkner (as I hail from the land of Christ), Hebrew myth in the stories of Borges and Singer (as I have pursued throughout to know the mystical, anti-rational side of Hasidism, the legend of Rabbi Loew who, in order to give life to the inert heap of clay, writes the Hebrew sign EMETH (truth) on its forehead—supposed to be that of Golem, then becomes a kind of servant and protector of the Ghetto), Aztec and Mayan myth in those of Carlos Fuentes, African Myth in those of Achebe and Chesnutt and the myth of the Old South in the stories of Caroline Gordon, a myth of rural New England in those of Sarah Orne Jewett, and the myth of success in those of F.Scott Fitzgerald and John O'Hara.

Perhaps more tenuous but possibly more rewarding too is that consideration of myth which focuses on archetypes. The term *archetype* is so widely in currency in recent years that if any character type or situation recurs twice, it is likely to have attributed to it a dimension of archetypicality ! I am referring here to the archetype in the Jungian meaning (as cited before) as a person, shape, or situation that could be recognised by people in any culture. Whether really of primordial origin (as Jung insisted), whether really a projection into the individual conscious from some "collective unconscious," it is, nevertheless, universal and no mere accident of time and place. The Hero, the Alter-Ego or Double, the Scapegoat, and the Trickster are among this psychic pantheon ; archetypal situations include the Quest (as in Suresh Joshi's short story '*Thingdu*' – 'The Patch' English translation), Transformation (of various kinds enumerated above in the gist of motifs), Initiation, Prophecy and Fulfilment etc.

All of the above-mentioned archetypal figures and situations are well represented in folktales – several hundred variants are devoted to the Quest, and there are 199 major Quest motifs (H 1200 through H 1399) which may appear in these or other tales. For whatever it might be worth, a similar quantification could be carried on for the other archetypal elements in folktales of the world.

To return to the thesis of this paper, let me say in brief that the folktale and our most popular and innovative literary form of to-day, the modern short story, derive from a common root, they are pointed towards the same goals, and they echo each other in mode, motif, and myth. Despite its evolution in new and strange and sometimes exciting directions, our short written tales, short story remains in the same genus with the tale of tradition.

Here ends our journey into the wonderland of folklore to-day. But we shall meet again, somewhere, sometime, to continue our mythical quest.

References

1. Cuddon, J.A., A Dictionary of Literary Terms (revised), New York, Penguin, rpt. 1985.
2. Campbell, Joseph (ed.), Portable Jung, Tr.R.F.C. Hull, New York; Penguin, rpt. 1977.

3. Jaffe, Aniele (ed.), Jung: Memories, Dreams, Re- flections, Tr.Richard and Clara Winston, London, Fontana Press, 1963.
4. Winternitz, M., A History of Indian Literature, New York: Russell and Russell, 1972.
5. Hanan, Patrick, The Chinese Short Story: Studies in Dating, Authorship and Composition, Cambridge : Harvard Univ. Press, 1973.
6. Tennyson, Alfred, The Poems and Plays of Alfred Tennyson, New York ; Random House, 1938.
7. Bynum, David, The Daemon in the Wood, Cambridge ; Harvard Uni. Press, 1978.
8. Harrison, James A. (ed.), The Complete Works of Edgar Allan Poe, XI ed.1902; New York ; AMS Press, 1965.
9. Auden, W.H.(ed.), 'Introduction,' Edgar Allan Poe : Selected Prose, Poetry and 'Eureka', New York, Rinehart, 1950.
10. Frye, Northrop, Anatomy of Criticism, Princeston; Princeston Univ. Press, 1957.
11. Arne, Antti and Stith Thompson, The Types of the Folktale, Helsinki, Academia Scientiarum Fennica, 1961.
12. Thompson, Stith, Motif – Index of Folk Literature, 6 Vols, Bloomington, Indiana Univ. Press, 1955-57.
13. Thompson, Stith and W.E. Roberts, The Types of the Indic Oral Tales : India, Pakistan and Ceylon, Helsinki, 1960.
14. Thalmann, Marianne, The Romantic Fairy Tale : Seeds of Surrealism, Ann Arbor : Univ. of Michigan Press, 1964.
15. Kostelanetz, Richard, "The Short Story in Search of Status," Twentieth Century, 174 (Autumn, 1965).
16. O'Connor, Frank, The Lonely Voice:A Study of the Short Story: Cleaveland; World, 1962.
17. Bowen, Elizabeth, The Faber Book of Modern Short (ed.) Stories, London; Faber & Faber, 1936.
18. Current Garcia, Eugene and Walton R. Patrick, Short Stories of the Western World, Chicago, Scott, Forseman, 1969.

19. Coleridge, Samuel, Biographia Literaria, London; Taylor Dent, 1947.
20. Walker, Warren S., Twentieth Century Short Story Explication, 3rd edn. Hamden ; Shoe String Press, 1977.
21. Voss, Arthur, The American Short Story, Norman; Univ. of Oklahoma Press, 1973.
22. Swink, Helen, 'William Faulkner : The Novelist as Oral Narrator', Georgic Review, 26, 1972.
23. Burrows, David (ed.), Myth & Motif in Literature, New York : Free Press, 1973.
24. Jarrell, Randell, A Sad Heart at the Supermarket, New York; Atheneum, 1962.
25. Evans, Oliver and Harry Finestone (eds.), The World of the Short Story: Archetypes in Action, New York ; Knof, 1971.
26. Matthews, Jack (ed.), Archetypal themes in the Modern Story, New York; St. Martin's Press, 1973.
27. Cummins, Walter M., The Other Side of Reality : Myths, Visions, and Fantasies, San Francisco ; Boyd & Fraser, 1972.
28. Guerard, Wilfred L. (ed.), Mandala : Literature for Critical Analysis, New York; Harper and Row, 1970.
29. Cafferata, John (ed.), Rites, New York : McGraw Hill, 1975.
30. Seltzer, Thomas (ed.), Best Russian Short Stories, New York ; The Modern Library, Random House, 1925.

Glossary of Dilectical and Other Terms

Adhibas	:	The night of the adhibas has been compared with the night of the ninth day of the lunar fortnight of the Bengali month of Aswin (nabami - nisi) – The marriage songs of ornamentation of the bride's mother and bride-groom's mother are sung on this night.
Aghon	:	Month of November-December when the paddy is ready for harvesting.
Akash	:	Space, one of the five universal elements.
Alapalava	:	In the enactment of the dance-drama based on the life of god Krishna in Manipur (India), one of the gestures used by young women from the complex system of hand gestures known as *mudras*. *Alapalava* is one such *mudra* performed by a rotation of the wrist accompanied by folding and unfolding of fingures to suggest trembling leaf.
Ananta	:	'Endless', the serpent on whom Vishnu sleeps or is seated.
Ashar	:	One of the Hindu months called *Aswin.*
Avadan	:	The Indian *Jatakas,* stories of the many reincarnations of Buddha, began to appear in written texts in the Sixth Century BC, and from *Jatakas* grew a related but more secular form called Avadana.

Behula	:	A well-known mythical character of Hindu Purana. Her story of devotion and dedication to her husband, the tragedy of her husband's death, and her subsequent grim endeavour to regain life for him is the theme of many songs, ballads and stories.
Bhakats	:	Brahmins attached to Satras in Assam–dedicated to religious performances.
Bihu	:	Assamese great festival.
Biyar git	:	Assamese marriage songs.
Chhatim	:	In Tripura, Alstonia Scholaris tree the top of which remains flat.
Clan	:	Families holding together and claiming descent from a common ancestoral lineage in tribal groups.
Dao	:	One type of cutting bill (weapon) produced by Naga blacksmiths. Decorated ones are meant for ceremonial occasions.
Daodi	:	Egg considered to be the symbol of creation of Dimasas (Hill Kacharis) of Assam.
Dar	:	Deepest portion of water.
Darai	:	A female deity worshipped in districts of Cachar (Assam) and Sylhet (Bangladesh).
Deoghanty	:	Costly bell worth hundreds of rupees used for decorative purpose by Hillmiris.
Desi	:	Native.
Devi	:	The Goddess, incorporating both benign and fearsome aspects.
Dhangar bassa	:	In each village of the Oraons and the Bhuiyas, there is an open space for a dancing ground called the '*Darbar*', and near it the 'bachelor's hall,' a separate house, for the young men, which is called the 'Dhangar bassa' or '*Mandarghar*' as here the young men, 'Dhangar', must all sleep at night, and here the drums, '*Mandar*,' are kept.

Dhangarin bassa	:	Like 'Dhangar bassa,' some of the villages have a 'Dhangarin bassa', or house for maidens, which they are allowed to occupy without any one to look after them. The maidens appear to have very great liberty in such house.
Digather	:	The Dimasa Kacharis put copper and gold in a pot of water and call it digather, i.e. pure water, and they purify themselves by touching the digather.
Dimasa	:	Great-River-Folk (di means "river or "water",) People who were driven out of the valley of the great water.
Dikki	:	A cultural hero of Garo people.
Doini-Pollo	:	Sun-Moon God in the Mythology of Minyongs(a section of the Adi tribe of Arunachal Pradesh).
Dormitory	:	In Konyak villages, there were sleeping quarters of unmarried girls, where the adult unmarried girls of several families congregated and, often spent the nights and even received the visits of young men.
Dura	:	Hard-shelled tortoise.
Dyaya Prithvi	:	The Heaven and Earth as called in Rig Veda. Not unlike the myths of the Adis and the Akas of Arunachal Pradesh, the sky and earth, *Dyaya - Prithvi* are conceived as compound deities, *Pitara, matara, janitri,* besides being separately addressed as 'father' and 'mother' in the Vedic conception *'rodasi.'*
Dyus Pitar	:	Sky-father found in Vedic Scripture.
En	:	Gold in Hillmiri dialect.
Ganga	:	Goddess, personification of the Ganges river.
Gawang	:	In the language of Wakching in Konyak area, the name of their deity is Gawang. Gawang means literally "Earth-Sky" and

		reflects the idea of a universal deity comprising or dominating both spheres of the world. To the Konyaks, the name Gawang denoted not the spiritual essence of the universe but a deity of highly personal character associated with the sky more than with the earth.
Gosain	:	Caste of Brahmin among Assamese people.
Hiranyagarbha	:	The Golden Egg, or Womb.
Kalicipad	:	The oldest form of folk song of Miris on love.
Kamkeli	:	Love-act.
Kanchan flower	:	Golden flower or Sun flower.
Kanya biday	:	Giving a send-off to the bride after marriage. *Kanya biday* rites are performed by Bengalee Hindus.
Kathakali	:	Fascinating classical form of musical dance-drama of Kerala recognised as a kind of new genre, as it contains the elements of both the dance and drama.
Katta Agana	:	Narrative folksong of Garo people.
Khamba	:	The Son of the hero of Moirang. Khamba and Thoibi, two lovers, regarded as deities, personify ideal Meithei hero and woman in Manipur.
Khulang Ishei	:	Song at the time of help in work.
Khunung Ishei	:	Archaic Song (ancient song) related to the past.
Kili	:	Rite of pledge between the bride and groom among Mundas in which a cup of beer is given to each ; the groom pours some of the contents of his cup into the bride's cup, and she returns the compliment. Drinking the liquor thus blended, they become of one 'Kili', that is the bride is admitted into her husband's tribe and they become one.
Kimbu	:	One of the Naga dances.

Kolokumari	:	A female deity worshipped by the Gangars, a fishing tribe of lower Bengal.
Konyak	:	Derivative of Keniak meaning "man" in the language of a small number of villages in Konyak area.
Krishna	:	Pastoral hero and amorous lover of Radha; as the supreme lord is an incarnation of Vishnu and Preacher of the *Bhagwad Gita*.
Kshatriya	:	Ruling warrior aristocracy in Hindu society.
Kshetra-devata	:	*Naga,* guardian of the fields.
Kujum Chantu	:	A mythical giantess found in the myth of the Apa Tanis of Arunachal Pradesh.
Laho	:	A dance form of Jaintias.
Lai Haraoba	:	Manipuri dance ritual (merry-making of gods), particularly of Methis.
Laukik	:	Earthly.
Lingang	:	A festival like Bihu celebrated by Miris.
Lokayana	:	Indian equivalent term of folklore coined by Suniti Kr. Chatterji, expressing the real scope of folklore as it signifies the way of life (*yana*) of a people (*loka*).
Lungterok	:	Six stones (lung means stone and terok means six). According to Ao Naga legend, the ancestors of Aos, Semas and Changs emerged from Lungterok of Chungliyimti village.
Mala Pujari	:	Recognised priest of local mother-deity in South India.
Mangalacaran	:	Ceremony performed on the auspicious occasion when the marriage is settled among Bengalee Hindus of Cachar district of Assam.
Manasa	:	Goddess of snakes; the cult of Manasa probably originated in Bengal and is still largely confined to eastern India. She is, by association, a goddess of fertility , and may be prevailed upon to cure snake bite.

Manasa Mangal	:	Recitals performed on the occasion of Manasa worship in Cachar-Sylhet districts particularly in the month of *Shravana,* the month sacred to Manasa.
Mandala	:	Geometric design of cosmic order. Used in conjuction with *bijas* in meditation.
Mandarghar	:	Bachelor's hall
Marchen	:	Fairy tale primarily a narrative genre of Indo-European peoples, which diffused into other cultures.
Marg	:	A creed.
Mauzadar	:	Land surveyor
Melo	:	Earth
Moirang Sayon	:	Manipuri epic having seven epic cycles concerning seven incarnations (sayon) of two lovers of Moi-lang.
Morung	:	Division of a village which in anthropological usage is described as ward corresponding to the morung, and in Konyak usage the morung names applied both to the actual men's houses and to the wards of which they were the focal points.
Moshup	:	Bachelors' dormitory among Adis of Arunachal Pradesh.
Mudra	:	Hand gesture indicating a specific mood or action -protection, compassion, meditation, teaching etc.
Murkonats	:	Silver
Nabami-nisi	:	Ninth day of the lunar fortnight of the Bengali month of *Aswin.*
Naga	:	Protective snake or snake spirit often taking a hybrid human-animal form.
Naga-kals	:	Snake-stones, engraved with intertwined snakes, are erected in clusters beneath sacred trees by women desiring children in southern part of India.
Nara	:	Green straw
Ojha	:	Originally village medicine men believed to be capable of curing snake bites in

contiguous districts of Cachar(Assam) and Sylhet (Bangladesh). They are popularly known as another class of people ministering Manasa deity for recital of *Manasa Mangal.*

On-bou : One kind of tree having red leaves.
Ongngo : Local name of a bird like weaver bird.
Pabibari : Bigman's house.
Padma : Lotus
Pan : Betel-nut,chewed rather as tobacco is also the price of the bride being paid in kind or cash among Kolhans, Mankis, Hos, Mundas and other tribes in Singbhum, Chutia Nagpur etc.
Parvati : 'Daughter of the Mountains', consort of Shiva, embodiment of peace and beauty.
Prakriti : Primeval matter identified with the female principle - energy, vitality and diversity. Counter- part of *purusha.*
Prajapati : Creator of the Universe identified with Brahma.
Pralaya : Undifferentiated Cosmic matter.
Pralaya - payadhi : Great deluge as per Hindu mythology recalling to mind the Biblical story.
Pratityasamutpada : Momentariness of the Buddhist theology.
Prithvi : Earth
Purush : Primeval Man ; male creative principle, counter-part of *prakriti.*
Purusha Shukta : Macro cosmic idea of the world as a vast personage echoing in the Rig Veda.
Radha : Consort of Krishna, his favourite *gopi.*
Rasheng : Girls' dormitory
Rig Veda : Early collection of hymns used at sacrifices embodying the religious beliefs of the Indo-Aryans.
Rupie : Ceremonial meat in Angami dialect.
Samaskars : Rituals and rites.
Satras : Religious institutions in Assam like Vaishnavite institutions in Manipur.

Saturnalia : Kachari festival. The April Bihu, the origin of which is still somewhat obscure, seems to be a 'Saturnalia' of much more objectionable character. During this festival, people abandon themselves freely to drunkenness and other forms of licentiousness , and cases of serious assault and riot have been known to accompany these gatherings.

Sedi : Sky

Shakta : Worshipper of the Goddess.

Shakti : Active energetic aspect of a god, sometimes personified as his wife.

Shravan : Hindu sacred month

Shiv : Hindu god characterised by his cosmic energy manifested in many creative and destructive forms.

Shri : Goddess (Lakshmi), consort of Vishnu.

Sirkar : Government

Sulapani : God worshipeed by Bengalee Hindus inhabiting Cachar district of Assam.

Tal : Cymbal.

Tamasha : Classical form of musical dance-drama of Maharastra.

Tantric : Cults and sects worshipping goddesses with magical ceremonies.

Tangaloa : God of heaven found in the mythologies of Hawaii, Society Island and Tahiti. The story repeated in their mythologies is that Tangaloa who was a prisoner for long ages in a gigantic egg, finally broke out of his confinement and created heaven and earth from the two halves of the shell. Such archetypal conception is not confined to rude tribes only.

Tuara Nangapa : Poetic art of *Katta Agana,* narrative song of Garos.

Thoibi : Princess Thoibi was the niece of the king

of Moirang in Manipur. Thoibi met Khamba by chance and they fell in love with each other. But the love affair was vitiated by mistaken identity. She killed Khamba who wanted to test her fidelity in disguise, she committed suicide.Both are worshipped as deities by Meitheis.

Upanayan : A ceremony of initiation in which the young boy receives the sacred thread, in the elaborate ritual that is viewed as a second birth in India. Baptism in early Christianity, Yog in India, and the complex puberty rituals among North American Indian cultures are similar examples of rebirth in rites of passage.

Upanishads : Philosophical and mystical texts.

Vaishnavite : Pertaining to Vishnu; worshipper of Vishnu.

Vedas : Ancient religious texts of the Indo-Aryans; see *Rig Veda*.

Vedic : Pertaining to the pre-Hindu, Indo-Aryan culture whose members compiled the *Vedas*.

Vishnu : Hindu god associated with creation and preservation myths; his various incarnations restore the balance of cosmic forces which sustain the universe.

Wangla : Folk dance of Garos.

Yama : Ruler of the dead.

Yamuna : Goddess, personification of the Jumuna river.

Zeus - Pater : Sky-father worshipped among the ancient Greeks. This conception of sky-father is no other than the Vedic *Dyus - Pitar*.

Bibliography

1. Aarne A.A. and Stith Thompson : The Types of the Folktale, 2nd rev. ed., trans. and enl. by Stith Thompson, Helsinki, Academia Scientiarum Fennica, 1961.
2. Ao, Alemchiba : Arts and Crafts of Nagaland, Kohima, Naga Institute of Culture, 1968.
3. Arokianathan, S. : Tangkhul Folk-Literature, 1982.
4. Auden, W.H. (ed.) : "Introduction,' Edgar Allan Poe : Selected Prose, Poetry and Eureka, New York ; Rinehart, 1950.
5. Banerjee, Projesh : The Folk Dances of India, Allahabad ; Kitabistan, 1944.
6. Banerjee, J.N. : The Development of Hindu Iconography, Calcutta ; 1956.
7. Barkakati, Anand Devi : Biyanam (n.d.), Jorhat ; 1948 - Assamese Songs.
8. Barakakati, S. : Tribes of Assam, New Delhi; National Book Trust of India, 1969.
9. Barth, A. : The Religion of India, 1932.
10. Bareh, H. : Khasi Fables & Folktales, 1971.
11. Barua, Hamchandra : Marriage Customs of the People of Assam (n.d.), Gauhati, 1892.
12. Barua, Hem : Folk Songs of India, New Delhi ; Indian Council of Cultural Relations, 1964.

13. Barua, P.K. : Kamrupiya Biya Geet (Marriage Songs of Kamrup), 1945.

14. Barua, T.K.M. : Wancho Love Songs, Itanagar ; Govt. of Arunachal Pradesh, Directorate of Research, 1982.

15. Baruah, K.L. : Human Sacrifice in Assam, Journal of the Assam Research Society, V.6, 1938.

16. Bascom, W.R. : Ifa Divination: Communication Between Gods and Men in West Africa, 1969.

17. Benfey, Theodore : Panchtantra, Berlin (in German), 1859.

18. Bhattacharya, P.C. : Boro Songs on Love ; Indian Folklore, (II.I) 1957.

19. —— : Glimpses from Boro Folk Songs, 1959.

20. Bhattacharya, P.K. : Folktales from Nagaland, Kohima ; Naga Institute of Culture, 1972.

21. Bompas, Cecil Henry : Folklore of the Kolhan, JAS Ben, L XXI, 1902 - Ballads, Tales, Proverbs, Ho.

22. Bordoloi, Dharamaram : Tiwa Sampradayar Parichay, Jorhat ; 1965.

23. Borgohain, A.K. : Folktales of Nagaland, Manipur, Tripura, New Delhi ; Sterling Publishers, 1973.

24. —— : Folktales of NEFA, New Delhi ; Sterling Publsihers, 1977.

25. Borgohain, B.K. and Roy Chaudhury,P.C. (Eds.) : Folktales of Nagaland, Manipur, Tripura and Mizoram, New Delhi Sterling Publishers, 1985.

26. Borooah, J. : Folktales of Assam, Howrah, rpt, 1962.

27. Bowen, Elizabeth(Ed.) : The Faber Book of Modern Short Stories, London ; Faber and Faber, 1936.

28. Brahma, Mohini Mohan : Folk Songs of the Bodos, Gauhati; Gauhati University, 1960.

29. Briffault, Robert : The Mothers, Vol.II, London, 1927.

30. British Advisory Committee and Indian Advisory Committee : In the Image of Man, New Delhi; Vikas Publishing House Pvt. Ltd., 1982.

31. Brown, Rev. N. : Comparison of Indo-Chinese Languages, Journal of the Asiatic Society of Bengal, V.6, 1837.

32. Burrows, David (ed.) : Myth and Motif in Literature, New York ; Free Press, 1973.

33. Burton, Robert : Anatomy of Melancholy, 1961.

34. Cafferata, John (ed.) : Rites, New York ; McGraw - Hill, 1975.

35. Chadwick, N. and Chadwick, H.M. : The Growth of Literature, 3 Vols., 1932-40.

36. Chatman, Seymour : Story and Discourse, Ithaca and London ; Cornell University Press, 6th edn., 1993.

37. Chatterji, Suniti Kumar : The Cultural Heritage of India, Vol.I, 1948.

38. Chattopadhyay, K. : Tribalism in Inda, New Delhi; Vikas Publishing House Pvt. Ltd., 1978.

39. Chaudhury, J.N. : A Comparative Study of Adi Religion, 1971.

40. Clark, Keneth and Mary : Introducing Folklore, New York ; Holt, Rinehart and Winston, 1963.

41. Coomarswamy, Anand K. : The Dance of Shiv : Fourteen Indian Essays; New Delhi; Munshiram Manoharlal 1974.

42. Crooke, W. : The Popular Religion and Folk-lore of Northern India, Vol.II, rpt., Delhi, 1968.

43. Culler, Jo nathan : Structuralist Poetics ; Structuralism, Linguistics and the Study of Literature , London ; Routledge & Kegan Paul, 1975.

44. Cummins, Walter M. : The Other Side of Reality :Myths, Visions and Fantasies, San Francisco, Boyd and Fraser, 1972.

45. Current - Garcia, Eugene and Walton R. Patrick : Short Stories of the Western world, Chicago; Scott, Foresman, 1950.

46. Dalton, Edward Tuite : Tribal History of Eastern India, New Delhi; Cosmo Publications, rpt. 1978.

47. Degh, L. : Folktales and Soceity, 1969.

48. Dell, Hymes (Ed.) : Language in Culture and Society, New York; Harper and Row, 1964.

49. Desai, Dr.Dewangana : Erotic Sculpture of India : A Socio-Cultural Study, New Delhi, 1975.

50. Directorate of Art and Culture, Kohima, Nagaland : Folktales from Nagaland,Vol.I & II, Dimapur, Nagaland.

51. Dorson, R.M. : Introduction to Folklore and Folklife : An Introduction, Chicago; Chicago University Press, 1972.

52. —— : American Negro Folktales, 1967.

53. —— : American Folklore, 1959.

54. Dundes, Allan (Ed.) : The Study of Folklore, New Jersy; Prentice Hall, 1965.

55. —— : Introducation to "The Morphology of the Folktale," 2nd edn, 1968.

56. —— : The Study of Folklore in Literature and Culture : "Identification and Interpretation" in Analytical Essays in Folklore, the Hague; Mouton.

57. —— : Structural Typology in North American Indian Folktales, Indiana University, 1965.

58. Durkheim, Emile : The Elementary Forms of Religious Life, 1915

59. Edgerton, Franklin : Panchatantra (tr. from Sanskrit), New Delhi; Orient Paperbacks, 1965.

60. Eliade, Mircea : Birth and Rebirth, 1958.

61. Endle, S. : The Kachari, New Delhi; Cosmo Publication, 1975 .

62. Ering, Oshong : 'Some Adi Myths,' NEFA Information, March, 1965.

63. Evans, Oliver and Harry Finestone (Eds.) : The World of the Short Story : Archetypes in Action, New York; Knoff, 1971.

64. Evans - Partichard, E.E. : Theories of Primitive Religion, 1965.

65. Fontenrose, Joseph E. : The Ritual Theory of Myth, 1966.

66. Forbes, C.J.F.S. : On Tibeto-Burman Languages, Journal of the Royal Asiatic Society of Great-Britain and Ireland, New Series, Vol.10, 1878.

67. Frazer, J.G. : The Golden Bough : A Study in Magic and Religion, 12 Vols., London, 1880.

68. —— : The Golden Bough (abridged), London, 1963.

69. —— : The Aftermath, London, 1936.

70. Freud, Sigmund : Jokes and Their Relation to the Unconscious, London; Hogarth Press, 1960.

71. —— : Totem and Taboo, London, 1950.

72. —— : Interpretation of Dreams, Vol.4, Penguin, 1976.

73. —— : The Occurrence in Dreams of Material from Fairy Tales, Standard Ed., 12, 281, 1913.

74. —— : With Oppenheim, D.E., Dreams in Folklore, New York ; Part I, Standard Ed., 12, 177, 1958.

75. Funk and Wagnall : Funk and Wagnall's Standard Dictionary of Folklore, Vols. 2, 1949-50.

76. Furer - Haimendorf Christoph VON : The Naked Nagas, London ; Metheun, 1932; Calcutta, Thacker, Spink & Co., rpt. 1962.

77. —— : Return to the Naked Nagas, New Delhi; Vikas Publishing House, 1976.

78. —— : The Konyak Nagas,New York; Holt,Rinehart & Winston, 1969.

79. —— : The Megalithic Culture of the Naga Tribes of Assam, Research and Progress, V.5, 1939.

80. —— : "Religious Beliefs and Ritual Practices of the Minyong Abors of Assam, India (Anthropos VI 49) 1954.

81. —— : The Apa Tanis and Their Neighbours,London; Routledge, 1962.

82. —— : Morals and Merit, London ; Weidenfeld and Nicolson, 1967.

83. —— : The Role of Songs in Konyak Culture, Man in India, 23 : 69-82, 1943 - A Collection and Interpretation of Konyak Songs.

84. Frye, Northrop : Anatomy of Criticism,Princeston; Princeston University Press, 1957.

85. Gargi, Balwant : Folk Theatre of India;University of Washington Press, 1966.

86. Gillin, John : The Ways of Men, New York, 1948.

87. Gorer, G . : Death, Grief and Mourning in Contemporary Britain, London, 1965.

88. Goswami, Prafulla Datta : Folk Literature of Assam, Gauhati, 1965.

89. —— : Ballads and Tales of Assam, Gauhati, University of Gauhati, 1960.

90. —— : Miri Folk Songs, IFL, II : 2, 1959 -

91. —— : Spring time Bihu of Assam, (A Socio-Cultural Study), Lawyer's Book Depot, Gauhati, 1966.

92. —— : The Bihu Songs of Assam, Gauhati; Lawyer's Book Stall, 1957.

93. —— : Bohen Bihu of Assam and Bihu Songs, Gauhati; The Assam Publication Board,1988.

94. —— : Naga Tales, Eastern Anthropologist, Vol. 8, No.2, December, 1954, Feb.1955.

95. —— : Kachari Ballads and Folk Songs, The Hindustan Standard, Oct. 14, 1945.

96. Griffith, R.T.H. : The Hymn of the Rigveda, Vol.II, Benaras, 1926.

97. Grimmes, G.E. : The Thread of Discourse, The Hague ; Jarina Lingnaran, 1979.

98. Grimwood, Ethel St.Clair : My Three years in Manipur, Delhi; Vivek Publishing House, rpt. 1975.

99. Grove : Grove's Dictionary of Music and Musicians, 5th ed., 1955.

100. Guerard, Wilfred L.(Ed.) : Mandala : Literature for Critical Analysis, New York ; Harper and Row, 1970.

101. Hanan, Patrick : The Chinese Short Story : Studies in Dating, Authorship and Com-

position, Cambridge ; Harvard Univ. Press, 1973.

102. Harris, Marvin : Rise of Anthropological Theory, London ; Routledge and Kegan Paul, 1972.

103. Harrison, James A. (Ed.): The Complete Works of Edgar Allan Poe, XI ed., rpt. New York; AMS Press, 1965.

104. Hastings, James (Ed.) : Encyclopaedia of Religion and Ethics, New York; Vols.5 (Ed. 1971-1973.)

105. Hawkes, Terence : Structuralism and Semiotics, London; Methuen,1977.

106. Hudson, J.H. : The Metheis, London; David Nutt, 1908.

107. Hudson, Thomas Callan : Head Hunting Among the Hill Tribes of Assam; Folklore, Vol. 20, 1909.

108. Hooke, S.H. (Ed.) : Myth, Ritual and Kingship, 1958.

109. Hsu, Francis L.K. : Religion, Science and Human Crisis, London, 1952.

110. Hutton, J.H. : The Sema Nagas (with a forward by Henry Balfour), London ; MacMillan, 1921; 2nd Edn. Bombay Oxford University press,1969.

111. —— : The Angami Nagas, 2nd edn. Bombay Oxford University Press, 1969.

112. —— : Diaries of Two Tours in Unadministered Area: East of the Naga Hills; Delhi, Gian Publishing House, 1986.

113. —— : Seven Folk Tales Collected by C.R. Pawsey from the Angami Nagas, FL, 1922.

114. —— : "Folktales of the Angami Nagas of Assam," FL(L), XXV, 4, (1914).

115. —— : "Folktales from the Naga Hills of

Assam", FL(L),XXXIV, (1923).

116. —— : A Primitive Philosophy of Life, 1938.

117. —— : "Two Angami Naga Songs", Manl, XXIII, (1943). Songs : Angami.

118. Hymes, Dell (Ed.) : Language in Culture and Society, Harper and Row; New York, 1964.

119. Imti, Aier L. : Ao Naga Social and Customary Geneology, Mokokchung ; The Pioneer Book Stall, 1969.

120. Ions, Veronica : Indian Mythology, London, 1967.

121. Jastrov, Joseph : Freud : His Dream and Sex Theories, New York; Simon and Schuster, Inc., 1969.

122. Joshi, Mahesh : Assam, The Indian Conflict, New Delhi; Prachi Prakashan, 1981.

123. Jung, C.G. : 'The Concept of the Collective Unconscious, (1936), 'The Phenomenology of the Spirit in Fairy Tales', (1945/1948), and 'On the Psychology of the Trickster-Figure'(1954), in Collected Works,Vol.IX, 'Archetypes and the Collective Unconscious', London; Routledge and Kegan Paul, 1948-55.

124. Kakati, Banikanta : Visnuite Myths and Legends, Gauhati, 1952.

125. —— : Mother Goddess Kamkhya, Gauhati.

126. Kalachand : Khamba Thoibi, Imphal ; O.K. Store, 1963.

127. Kauff Mann, Walter : Songs of the Naga Hills, Micro Bibliotheka Anthropos, No.4, Possins Frieburg, 1953.

128. Kirti Sing, Dr.M. : Folk Culture of Manipur, Delhi ; Manas Publications, 1993.

129. Kostelanetz, Richard : The Short Story in Search of Status, Twentieth Century, 174, Autumn, 1965.

130. Kroebar, A.L. : Anthropology, (revised edn.), 1948.

131. —— : The Nature of Culture, Chicago, 1952.

132. Kumar, Dr.B.B. : Folklores and Folklore Motifs, New Delhi ; Omsons Publications, 1993.

133. —— : Modernization in Naga Society, New Delhi; Omsons Publications, 1993.

134. Lannoy, Richard : The Speaking Tree : A Study of Indian Culture and Society, London/New York, 1971.

135. Lazlo, Halasz (ed.) : Literary Discourse : Aspects of Cognitive and Social Psychological Approaches, Berlin, 1987.

136. Lawson, J. : European Folk Dance, 1953.

137. Leach, Maria (ed.) : The Standard Dictionary of Folklore, Mythology and Legend, New York, 1949-50.

138. Lekis. L. : Folk Dances of Latin America, 1958.

139. Lessa A. William, and Evon Z. Vogt. : Reader in Comparative Religion : An Anthropological Approach, 1958.

140. Levi-Straus, Claude : Structural Anthropology, Vol.2, Penguin, 1973.

141. Lewis, C.S. : A Grief Observed, London ; Faber, 1961.

142. Linton, Ralph : The Study of Man, New York, 1936.

143. Lomax, Alan : Folk Song Style and Culture, 1968.

144. Lord, A.B. : The Singer of Tales, 1960.
145. Lowie, Robert H. : Primitive Religion, 1936.
146. Lukacs, George : The Meaning of Contemporary Realism, London ; Merlin Press, 3rd ed., 1972.
147. Luikam, R. : Naga Folktales, New Delhi; Select Books, 1983.
148. —— : Folklore and Tales of the Nagas, New Delhi; Emmanuel Publishers - Printers, 1987.
149. Lyall, Sir Charles : The Mikirs, London, 1908.rpt., Gauhati, United Publishers.
150. Macdonell, A.A. : A Vedic Reader for Students, 1960.
151. Macdonell, A.A. and A.K. Keith : Vedic Index of Names and Subjects, Vols. 1 & 2, 1912.
152. Mackenzi, A. : The North-East Frontier of India, Delhi, Mittal Publications, rpt., 1979.
153. Mackenzi, D.A. : Myths from China and Japan, London, 1930.
154. Majumdar, D.N. : Tribal Situation in India, Simla, 1972.
155. Mathews, Jack(ed.) : Archetypal Themes in the Modern Short-Story, New York; St. Martin's Press, 1973.
156. Mead, Margaret (Ed.) : The Study of Culture at a Distance, Chicago, 1953.
157. Merwin, Harris : The Rise of Anthropological Theory; London, Routledge and Kegan Paul, 1972.
158. Middleton, John (Ed.) : Gods and Rituals, 1967.
159. Mills, J.P. : The Ao Naga, (with a forward by Henry Balfour), London, Macmillan,1926; (reprint) Bombay Oxford University Press, 1973.
160. —— : The Lotha Naga,(with an Introducation by J.H.Hutton), London, Macmillan,1922; (2nd edn)

Directorate of Art and Culture, Govt. of Nagaland, 1980.

161. —— : Folk Stories in Lhota Naga, New Delhi, Gian Publishing House, 1987.

162. —— : The Rengma Nagas, London, McMillan 1937 - Chapters on Folklore and language.

163. Miranda, P. and Miranda, E. (Ed.). : Structural Analysis of Oral Traditions, University of Pensylavania, 1971.

164. Miri, Sujata (Ed.) : Religion and Society of North East India, Delhi, Vikas Publishing House Pvt. Ltd., 1980.

165. Mitchell, J.Mury : Specimen of Wedding Songs of the Munda Kolhs, I. Ant. IV, 1875 - Songs, Mundari.

166. Mitra, Bahadur P.K. : Mundari Folktales, Ranchi, 1957.

167. Munda, R.D. : Cultural Elements in Ho Folk Songs, Calcutta, Indian Publications, 1971

168. Murry, Grace A. : Ancient Rites and Ceremonies, London,1930.

169. Nath, R.M. : The Background of Assamese Culture, Gauhati, 1978.

170. Neog, Maheswar : Swararekhat Borgeet, Assam Sangeet Natak Academy, Shillong, 1958.

171. Norbeck, Edward : Religion in Primitive Society, 1961.

172. Oldhan, C.F. : Serpent Worship in India, Journal of the Royal Asiatic Society of Great Britain and Ireland, 1891.

173. Parkes, Colin Murray : Bereavement : Studies of Grief in Adult Life, New York, Penguin, 1972.

174. Pawsey, C.R. : Ten Folk Stories in Sema Naga, JRAS Ben, V(1939)- Tales : Sema (Naga).

175. Pawsey C.R. and J.H.Hutton : "Folktales from the Naga Hills of Assam" FL(L), XXXIII, (1922).
176. Philips, J.L. : Folklore of the Santals, Orientals, I, 1884-Tales ; Santali.
177. Pike, E.R. : The Strange Ways of Man, New York, 1967.
178. Playfair, A.L. : The Garos ; London, 1909, Reprint ,Gauhati, 1975.
179. Prakashi, Mira : Folktales of Assam, New Delhi, Sterling Publishers, 1970.
180. Prasad, Dineswar : Hoffman on Mundari Poetry : Patna, Jyoti, 1979.
181. Propp, V.A. : Morphology of the Folktale, Austin, University of Texas Press, 1968. (Original in Russian, 1928); 2nd edn. Austin, 1970.
182. —— : Transformations in Fairy-tales in Maranda (ed.) Mythology, London, Penguin, 1972.
183. Rachlin, G. : Griefs and Discontents ; Boston, Little Brown, 1965.
184. Raglan, F.R.S. : The Hero : A Study in Tradition, Myth and Drama, 1956.
185. Raha, Manis K. : 'Folk Songs of the Tribals of West Bengal' in Folk Music and Folklore, Research Society, Calcutta, 1967 - Songs ; Bengali, Santali.
186. Ramanujan, A.K. (Ed.) : Folktales from India, New Delhi, Penguin Books of India, 1993.
187. Rafy, Mrs. : Folktales of Khasis.
188. Robinson, W. : Notes on the languages of various Tribes-inhabiting the valley of Assam and its Mountain Confines, JASB, XVIII, 1849.
189. Rongmuth, Dewansing : Folktales of the Garos, Gauhati University, 1960.
190. Roy, Sachin : Aspects of Padam-Minyong Culture, Shillong, North East Frontier Agency, 1966.

191. —— : 'Rhymes and Rhythms of the Abors' - IFL Dec.1957 - Songs ; Adi.

192. Roy, Sarat Chandra : "The Study of Folklore and Tradition in India", J.Bihar, ORS XVIII, 1982 - Tales, Songs, etc.

193. Sapir, E. : Culture, Language and Personality, Selected Essays, 1957.

194. Sarkar, R.M. : "Tribal Women Through Customs and Traditions" in Women in Indian Folklore, Indian Publications, Calcutta, 1969.

195. Seltzer, Thomas (ed.) : Best Russian Short Stories, New York ; The Modern Library, Random House, 1925.

196. Sharma, R.R.P. : The Sherdukpens, Shillong, N.E.F.A., 1960.

197. Shyam Choudhury, N.K. and M.M. Das : The Lalung Society, Calcutta, 1973.

198. Singh, E. Nilakanta : 'Manipur : A Land of Dance' IFL, II : 4(1961) - Songs, Dance, Drama : Manipuri.

199. Sinha, Raghuvir : Religion and Culture of North-Eastern India, New Delhi, Abhinav Publications, 1977.

200. Smith, William Carlson : Ao Naga Folktales, V. 37, 1926.

201. —— : The Ao Naga Tribes of Assam, A study in Ethnology & Sociology, London, MacMillan, 1925.

202. Sokolov, Y.M. : Russian Folklore, New York, MacMillan & Co. , 1950.

203. Spreen, H.L. : Folk Dances of South India, 1945.

204. Srivastav, L.R.N. : The Gallongs, Research Deptt., Advisers' Secretariat, Shillong, 1962.

205. Stevenson, Mrs. S. : The Rites of the Twice-Born, London, 1920.

206. Stone, Merlin : The Paradise Papers, London, 1977.

207. Strause, Claude Levi : Structural Anthropology, Vol-2, Penguin, 1973.

208. Stutley, Margaret, and James : A Dictionary of Hinduism, London, 1977.

209. Swink, Helen : "William Faulkner : The Novelist as Oral Narrator," Georgia Review, 26, 1972.

210. Taddei, Maurizio : Monuments of Civilization: India, London, 1977.

211. Thalmann, Marianne : The Romantic Fairy-Tale:Seeds of Surrealism, Ann Arbor, University of Michigan Press, 1964.

212. Thompson, Stith : Motif - Index of Folk Literature, 6 Vols, 2nd edn, Bloomington, Indiana University Press, 1955-58.

213. —— : A : Aarne, The Types of the Folktale, 2nd rev. edn., trans. and enl., F.F. Communication 184 ; Helinski, 1961.

214. —— : The Folktale, 1946.

215. —— : Tales of the North American Indians, 1929, reprinted 1966.

216. —— : With Jonas Balys ; The Oral Tales of India, Bloomington Indiana University Press, 1958.

217. —— : With Warren E.Roberts; Types of Indic Oral Tales, India, Pakistan and Ceylon, Helsinki, 1960.

218. Trigunayat, Jagdish : "Some Munda Songs (Collection from Bihar)" IFL, 1:3 (1958) - Songs, Munda.

219. Turner, W. Victor : The Forest of Symbols, 1967.

220. Upadhyay, Krishnadev,: and Sankar Sen Gupta Studies in Indian Folk Culture, Calcutta, Indian Publications, 1963.

221. Vatsayan, Kapil : Traditions of Indian Folk Dance, New Delhi, India Book Depot, 1976.

222. Verrier, Elvin : Myths of the North East Frontier of India, Shillong, North East Frontier Agency, 1968.

223. —— : A New Book of Tribal Fiction, Shillong, North East Frontier Agency, 1970.

224. —— : The Art of the North East Frontier of India, Shillong, N.E.F.A., 1959.

225. —— : A Philosophy for NEFA, Shillong NEFA, 1957.

226. —— : India's North East Frontier in the Nineteenth Century, New York, Oxford University Press, 1959.

227. Vickery, John and J'nan Sellery (Eds.) : The Scapegoat : Ritual and Literature, Boston, Houghton Mifflin, 1972.

228. Voss, Arthur : The American Short Story, Norman, University of Okhlahoma Press, 1973.

229. Walker, Warren S. : Twentieth Century Short Story - Explication, 3rd edn, Hamden, Shoe String Press, 1977 ; and Supplement I to third edition, 1980.

230. Whitehead, H. : The Village Gods of South India, Calcutta, 1921.

231. Wilgus, D.K. : Anglo-American Folksong Scholarship since 1898. (1959)

232. Winterinitz, M. : A History of Indian Literature, Vol. 1& 2, 1927, 1933. Reprint New York, Russell and Russell, 1972.

Index